GOD THE TRICKSTER?

ELEVEN ESSAYS

QUAKER *Q* BOOKS

First published in June 2001 by Quaker Books
Friends House, Euston Road, London NW1 2BJ

ISBN 0-85245-327-2

Edited by Ben Pink Dandelion
Copy Editor: Peter Daniels
Designed & typeset by Jonathan Sargent
Text: Original Garamond 10.8 on 14pt
Printed by Thanet Press Ltd.

Contents

Introduction

Ben Pink Dandelion

Two of the most basic questions that face religious believers, it seems to me, are 'What is of God?' and 'What does God require of me?'

For Liberal Friends who have placed so much emphasis and authority on experience and continuing revelation, of God working and teaching in our everyday lives, the 'What is of God?' question is particularly acute. We no longer claim that all true revelation will be verified by scripture or tradition. We can be led in utterly new ways at any time. And we face this challenge of discernment daily, even hourly. There's a wonderful quotation in Britain Yearly Meeting's *Quaker Faith and Practice* from Violet Holdsworth about giving ministry in Meeting.

> Each Friend who feels called upon to rise and deliver a lengthy discourse might question himself and herself most searchingly as to whether the message could not be more lastingly given in the fewest possible words, or even through his or her personality alone in entire and trustful silence. Cream must always rise to the surface. True. But other substances rise to the surface besides cream. Substances which may have to be skimmed off and thrown away before bodies and souls can be duly

nourished. Is my message cream or scum? It may be an unusual and it may be a very homely query, still it's one that every speaker, in a crowded gathering especially, should honestly face. Some of the dangers of silent worship can best be guarded against by its courtesy (Britain YM 1995: 2.64).

So we need to ask of everything we do or say – is it cream or scum? Is it the will of God or not? This is a critical and recurring question. Is it of God?

Once certain of it being Divine, or, rather, less uncertain of it not being not-from-God, we then ask what it is that this new leading may require of us.

In *The Last Temptation of Christ* by Nikos Kazantzakis, translated into English by the Quaker Peter Bien, there are two bits that really spoke to me. Here is the first. The son of Mary has gone to a monastery in a desert. He gets there after a long journey.

> 'The Abbot is dying' said the monk. 'You've arrived too late my Brother. Go back.' 'God commanded me to come' the son of Mary replied. 'Is he capable of hoaxing his children?' The monk cackled. He'd seen a good deal in his lifetime and had no confidence in God. 'He's the Lord isn't he? So he does whatever comes into his head. If he wasn't able to inflict injustice, what kind of an omnipotent would he be?' (Kazantzakis 1987: 141)

If it is true that there's always the possibility of being tricked or hoaxed, this severely complicates matters. Is it from God? What does God have to say to me? Is God joking?

The second piece from Kazantzakis which spoke to me is where the Rabbi, who is dying, is having a dream.

> Everything is of God he reflected. Everything has two meanings. One manifest, one hidden. The people comprehend mainly what is manifest. They say this is a snake and their minds go no further, but the mind

which dwells in God sees what lies behind the visible and sees the hidden meaning (Kazantzakis 1987: 155). I feel I live that idea that everything has two meanings. Nothing is an accident. Nothing is a coincidence. But what if there are sometimes three meanings? The secular external, the hidden meaning we see at first from God, and a deeper-meaning-behind-the-holy-trick which we only find out later, if at all.

All of the authors in this collection subscribe to a personal relationship with God where such questions are important in daily life. Secondly, all have felt in some way or other a sense of being tricked along their spiritual paths. In some way, a Trickster figure has been at work in our lives.

As Andrew Samuels says:

> Trickster figures and stories appear in many cultures ... For the Greeks, the arch-Trickster was Hermes, with his tendency to play jokes, to lie, to cheat, to steal, to deny reality, and to engage in grandiose fantasy ... Genuine Tricksters, from Coyote in North America to Ananse or Eshu in West Africa, follow that pattern, undermining the prevailing organization of power and even the perceived structure of reality itself (Samuels 1993: 81).

One of the most studied Trickster stories is from the Winnebago Native Americans. Paul Radin's book on this, first published in Zürich in 1954, then in New York in 1956 (and reprinted in 1973), with a commentary by Carl Jung on the Trickster archetype, is referred to many times by the authors here. So is the book of Job in the Hebrew Scriptures, a book which appears to depict a God who plays games. Other writers have looked to Genesis to dispute who is tricking who (Niditch 1987, Bledstein 1993).

Today, Quakers, and other believers, have a problem with such a fickle God. In belief surveys, theist Friends prefer an all-loving and all-knowing God to one who is all-powerful (Dandelion 1996: 161). The problem of suffering is eradicated by not attributing omnipotence to a Divine figure who otherwise loves and knows, i.e. a God who would prevent suffering if only God could. In a way, the authors of this collection take a similar line. The Trickster is either not God but a malevolent 'other' or shadow-side or the Tricks we have experienced are benign games with moral intention; indeed some experience the Tricks as the only possible way God could have brought them back to a life of faithfulness. In these theologies, God is presented almost without choice, using only what means are necessary to help the lost individual.

Many of those Friends approached to write for this book claimed they had not had any experience of a Trickster God in their lives, others felt the episodes of such experience too personal or sensitive to write about. This book is a collection of the stories of eleven authors who didn't feel that way. All underwent clearness processes as to whether or not to contribute and the book itself is the result of this collective sense of leading. We hope we weren't being tricked!

❁

The book begins with a passage from **Chuck Fager** excerpted from a longer piece, 'Quakerism and the Tricky Way of Wisdom'. In these Wisdom texts, such as Job, Ecclesiastes, and the Book of Jonah, he writes:

> we find repeatedly the motif of God acting in human affairs in ways that are unpredictable and, from the human perspective at least, capricious or indeed, tricky (page 5).

Using different English translations of the Bible to help make his point, Chuck points to earlier acknowledgements of the Trickiness of God:

> Whenever I tried to become wise and learn what goes on in the world, I realized that you could stay awake night and day and never be able to understand what

God is doing. However hard you try, you will never find out. Wise men may claim to know, but they don't (Ecc. 8:16-17, TEV) (page 6).

Human 'wisdom' is an outward illusion when it comes to truly trying to know God. For Job, this game of God's is confusing and unjust. God's intentions are not so readily transparent to the human mind.

Jane Orion Smith in her 'Forever Fallen? Trickster and God-Centred Identity' covers and melds Aboriginal and Jungian perspectives on the Trickster before developing ways in which God might be thought of as Trickster. As other authors do later in the book, she quotes Radin on the Trickster archetype, and also outlines Jung's analysis of Trickster. Applying Radin and Jung to the story of James Nayler and of Nayler's exchanges with Fox prior to his ride into Bristol, she concludes:

> Nayler and Fox both fell prey to pranks of Trickster and their personal shadow in 1656 ... all became victims of their own actions and egos (page 23).

Up to this point in her essay, Trickster has been separate from ideas of God, but Jane Orion then turns to the question 'Can God be a Trickster?' and finds Job instructive.

> God struck an arrangement with Satan, clearly aware of the consequences – why else would he put a restriction on how far Satan could go in this? (page 28).

Jane Orion does not stop here, however. She concedes that life can feel 'full of tricks', and that God can use situations for good.

> Sometimes I can almost see a sly smile on God's face as I read this story or as I encounter my own misfortunes for I know – and God and Trickster know – that these are opportunities for transformation and refinement (page 28).

This view of God means theologically co-opting and changing the archetype to help explain experience. However, Jane Orion concludes that, different definitions of Trickster aside,

> these encounters with our own Trickster ... are really encounters with transformative energy and opportunity. They are not to be avoided but waded into and divined through (page 31).

And the playing out of these confusions and crises in our lives can be seen as moments of transformation, and greater personal and collective intimacy with God.

Jan Arriens in 'A Very Shabby Fellow' takes a slightly different approach. He suggests that God's initial and ultimate trick is to give us no certainty of God's existence, and the problem of suffering exacerbates the challenge of faith.

But there is a point to such Trickery, particularly in this present age of persistent individualism. This chapter examines how affliction can paradoxically help us transcend our sense of individuality, how we go through life facing two ways at once – the whole and the individual – and how God is essentially a Trickster because we tend to approach God only from the vantage point of the individual – especially in this age of individualism.

> Sin is the loss of innocence, the birth of individuality. It is this which needs to be sacrificed in order to wipe away the separation and merge again with the whole ... So searching for God is as elusive as the pot of gold at the end of the rainbow. It is not the seeker who will find. We seek something we will never find, to find something we never lost. It is because we are looking through the wrong end of the telescope that such paradox abounds (pages 42-43).

Our sense of individualism is an illusion and a delusion: it is this that Divine Trickery helps us overcome, and as the culture of individualism increases, so does God's trickery.

In these circumstances, it is not surprising that God becomes even more of a Trickster. But unlike Job, we do not even rail against God, but dismiss the whole concept as illusion (page 46).

Secularisation complicates matters further as God is not even part of the picture. God's trickery is thus stretched further into our lives, in an age 'of great potential for inner stress, confusion and ultimate unfulfilment – in short, for experiencing God as Trickster' (page 48). Again, Jan concludes with a positive intention for this Trickster God.

Kirsten Backstrom in 'A Perfect Paradox' also takes on the themes of paradox and suffering. She looks at the Trickster as a Divine Fool, like the Royal Fool, whose role

> was to test the limits of the King or Queen's tolerance, to taunt and tease, to dance with danger like a kitten toying with a lion's tail, even to behave shamefully – and through this behavior, with a paradoxical grace and eloquence, to 'speak truth to power' (page 53).

God the Trickster is in the paradoxes, great and small, that make up our lives. It is understanding this which can give us a key to greater understanding. At one level, it is ridiculous to ask the big 'what is life all about?' questions. Theology itself, this book even, can be seen as a misspent project. Paradox is experience shared amongst humanity even whilst our experiences are so varied and personal. Kirsten talks in particular in her chapter of her own experience of living and suffering with cancer diagnosis and treatment through this lens of paradox. Even in the face of mockery, Kirsten concludes that 'For me, having a life-threatening illness was an extraordinary opportunity' (page 56).

As for Jane Orion, the Trickster archetype is hard to fit with the Quaker God:

> Any conception of the divine must take the existence of ugliness and absurdity somehow into account. However, the God of pure Light that many Friends embrace does not wear the mask of Coyote easily ... From Job to Jesus, from the martyrs of history and myth to many more ordinary folks in modern times – the 'good' are the ones to suffer. But, there is another way to look at this paradox (pages 61, 63).

This other way is to be reminded of the 'glimpses' of the transcendent that sufferers like Kirsten have glimpsed *through* the very experience of suffering. This brings us back to Jan's apparently unloving God who allows the horrors of genocide and torture, and the reality that life involves death and loss, emotional and physical pain. Kirsten's way through the paradox and its meaning (and like Jane Orion, Kirsten uses Nayler as an example) is to return to the idea of God as Holy Fool. God is as God is to bring us to a greater sense of reality, for humanity to know itself as it really is, not, as for Jan, puffed-up with its own roles and responsibilities. This is a God who clearly wants to go beyond the outward meanings, and even the meanings so frequently attributed by theologians down the ages.

Gay Pilgrim in 'A Trail of Tricks' writes as someone who has had to come to terms with the whole of the religious enterprise, and who, slowly, has accepted that it may involve a God who plays tricks, perhaps even a series of them, in order for us to reach our potential and our calling. Continuing Kirsten's theme of paradox and Chuck's identification of Wisdom that looks more like Trickery, Gay writes:

> Even if the concept of God as Trickster and Hoaxer is inconceivable for some, I think it is indisputable that paradox is real, and paradox can often feel like being tricked or hoaxed (page 75).

Gay's story covers decades. This is the long-haul Trickster God, in on our lives for the bigger picture, interfering and intervening even when God's wishes are not clear to us. Gay has felt repeatedly 'woken up', not always to her amusement.

> But 'wake up' to what? Why does God seem to hit me over the head with a sledgehammer to get my attention, and then seemingly abandon me with my head spinning and aching, to work out 'what on earth that was all about'? (page 76).

Whether or not the Tricks have been part of a serial call or single leading is not yet clear to Gay but she comments on the cumulative effect: 'What happened for me was that I could no longer screen the void' (page 89).

> My life choices have finally brought me to a place, both physically and spiritually, where I can be broken open to this knowledge by God and changed by it. Perhaps I could have arrived here sooner, or more easily, but I suspect the journey I took was necessary for me and that in some deep recess of my soul I knew that (page 90).

Margery Post Abbott has found that the writing of her chapter, 'The Belly of the Whale', has itself increased her understanding of the concept of Trickster. In her piece, Margery looks back on how God broke through her protective shell to release creative energy and potential. She draws a compelling and finely crafted contrast between her own story and that of Jonah, about which she claims, 'Of the Bible stories, it perhaps comes closest to the Native American myths of the Trickster' (page 111).

Following Jane Orion's and Kirsten's discussions on reconciling the Winnebago Trickster with a Scriptural Trickery, Margery comments:

> Unlike the Winnebago stories, where the Trickster is foolish and has his conscience awakened, in Jonah, God

is both the Trickster and the one who seeks to teach (page 112).

This gives reason to God's playing with us. She concludes: 'It is no surprise that God has to take drastic steps to get my attention' (page 96). Significantly, for Margery the Trickster is both benign *and* offering an invitation. It is up to us how far we choose to respond.

Marti Matthews in 'God the Fox' concurs with the theme of God using Trickster means to break through our personal stubbornness.

> I have always dragged my feet through life's changes ...
> it may be my own stubbornness that has required God
> to open me up by turning my life upside down again and
> again (page 115).

Whether this has been an invitation may be less clear. Marti tells a story of great personal suffering and tragedy, of the untimely death of two husbands. She quotes Dag Hammarskjöld on self-surrender, as what it means 'not to look back', and 'to take no thought for the morrow' (page 120).

Following Jan and Margery, Marti emphasises the theme of community and collectivity. With Kirsten, she illustrates how our lives are not our own, and also how suffering may have some perverse purpose in this process of building up our awareness of these salient truths. For Marti, the Trickster is the Fox. It is the Fox who constantly requires us to act. A Fox who intervenes at key moments, a Trickster with a final agenda of non-individuality, of non-attachment – 'I have to hold onto things lightly' (page 125).

In a wry comment at the end of her chapter, and echoing some of what Jane Orion and more explicitly Jan have written, Marti suggests that the very concept of being tricked is a product of our lingering overgrown sense of importance and individualism, which may be

> as humorous to the Fox as is the self-seriousness of ants.
> Perhaps the Fox seems a Trickster to us only because we
> are being led by quite a different point of view (page 130).

In the face of the suffering and loss she has experienced, Marti's optimism is infectious and humbling. She concludes with such certainty and faith:

> The Fox and I will zig and zag and hurry forward till suddenly – still unexpectedly – I'll find us at the end, the goal for which I was born. Yes, there is still that *total* detachment to do. What trick will the Trickster have to come up with to persuade me to do this? (page 133).

My own chapter has an equal optimism, as if I am at least 'in on the game'. It has not been a necessarily pleasant experience but its resonance with that of Friends of an earlier generation is heartening. My story, 'Tricks and Angels', written in 1998 like many of the chapters in the book, follows the themes of Trickery countering ego and self. God was willing me to let go of myself,

> To realise 'I' am not what matters. And yet the journey described here is all about a 'me' I watch and observe and judge, and one I feel is judged by God (page 135).

Like many of the other authors, I write about God's tricks being 'a crucial part of "waking me up" to a truth beyond my own making ... with God using what has been most important in my own self-definition in order to get me towards a more Divinely-defined life' (*Ibid.*). The endpoint is about enlightenment and uncertainty, submission and obedience. This is a God we can only begin to understand and who may only stop playing tricks once we stop trying to be in control.

Michele Lise Tarter contributes a moving and dramatic piece, 'Walking Between the Worlds: The Divine Mystery and Trickery of Moab', about the death of her stepfather and how in typical Trickster chaos, she was led to travel into the desert at a key time in her academic life and into an adventure of equally extra-rational actions. She quotes Lewis Hyde on the Trickster as a 'boundary crosser' between the real and illusory, and continues: 'The trick ... is not arbitrary or erratic at all, but an intricate design which provokes us to break free from our world in order to see life anew' (page 160). We are stretched, revitalised, our belief systems are reaffirmed. In this particular story, the 'Trick' takes Michele to a new place, a place of wisdom, a place of renewed faith, a place of salvation. Nothing is an accident. Nothing has that single outward meaning. Like myself in the chapter before, we are left sensing the celebration of God choosing to work in our lives in this way.

Nat Kuhn offers a shorter piece, 'Trickster and the Power of Paradox' to this collection, also with that insider glint in his eye. Picking up the common theme of stubbornness, Nat then takes on a new theme, that of our own God-given tricksterness!

> If God is a Trickster, and if we are to do God's work on earth, then the syllogism suggests that we are called to be Tricksters, too (page 164).

Quaker stories are full of evidence for this – indeed Chuck leads off the whole book with one about 'wisdom fish' (page 2) – but it is as if Nat sees this as symbolic of a faithful life. It is part of our own self-help to move us into this space beyond the secular everyday, beyond the rational and ordered. In common with other authors, Nat ends on a celebratory note.

> When paradox works, it offers us a trap door out of our prison of words, and into the mystery that is the essence of the divine. And that is something truly worth celebrating (page 166).

The last chapter in the book, 'To Prosper You and Not to Harm You' is from **Seren Wildwood**. It tells of a faithful response to a vocation, in her case a call to be a mother, through years of trickery and uncertainty. God uses what is necessary to help us in our vocations, to help us remain close to God. After ten years of confusing and distressing struggle, Seren gave birth to Hannah.

Fourteen months later, Hannah was rushed to hospital with a brain tumour. At the time of Seren's writing, Hannah was undergoing chemotherapy and the prognosis was not good. Incredibly, it may seem, Seren was at peace in her prayers:

> Perhaps the Trickster's work is done: I was tested and accepted into my vocation, and it is not for me to specify the path thereafter (page 183).

It seemed to me right to end the book with such a testimony of faith in the face of such uncertainty and pain. As Seren herself concludes:

> 'For I know the plans I have for you,' declares the Eternal One, 'plans to prosper you and not to harm you, plans to give you hope and a future. When you call to me, and come and pray to me, I shall listen to you. When you search for me, you will find me' (Jer. 29: 11-13, NIV and JB) (page 185).

✸

This is a book about personal experience and the attempts to make sense of it. A book about theology. It is a book of experience that is at least startling and surprising for those who have lived through it, at most tragic, distressing, and full of pain.

What interests me is the optimism and hope which shines through the accounts. The faith that is maintained, sustained, and even reaffirmed through a God of tricks. Of course, we need to bear in mind three things. First, that this is a book written by those who felt they had something constructive to say about a Trickster God – many more may have had similar experiences and come out of them with far less optimism. They may still be in distress or have discounted Quakerism and/or God altogether as happens for many (Richter and Francis 1998: 34). Secondly, our Religious Society of Friends affirms the positive, and we as Quaker writers may feel a moral obligation or temperamental impulsion not to dwell on less favourable interpretations. Thirdly, as frail humans, we may have a psychological requirement to try and make some positive sense out of our bitter experiences. Other Quakers have Gods less involved in daily life, less likely to cause motorcycle accidents or worse, even if it is at the expense of not being able to rationalise the harder moments of life. Of course, all of the writers speak only from their experience. They talk of *their* God: even where some make personal sense of suffering, none goes so far as to say that all suffering has the same Divine intention as it has had in their own lives. Nevertheless, I feel and hope the positive outlook of the theology outlined here may offer some solace to those struggling to make experience of similar situations.

The other point that has come to me in writing this introduction is how often individualism or ego is the target of trickery. Many writers see how it is only a trick of the kind they experienced which could have brought them back closer to God, to their particular calling, but many too seem to be going further than that, to a point where the individual becomes secondary to being part of the people of God. This may appear in contradiction with the idea of personal call which each espouses, but where that call is about finding our place amidst the formation of a faithful people of God, the contradiction disappears. In this sense, this transatlantic collection of writers represents a particular kind of believer. With a personal God interested in daily life, with an openness to self-discipline or denial, and holding notions that all is potentially of God and from God, these Friends are not typical Liberal Quakers.

What I want to suggest is that there is much of the Quietist flavour of Quakerism in some of the accounts here. Kathryn Damiano's thesis (1988) on that period of Quakerism which lasted about 130 years talks much of the two questions I began with: What is of God? What does God require of me? Stories of couples waiting 23 years to marry in order to be sure that their match is of God are memorable in this context. The difference between that period and now is the lack of anxiety the writers here exhibit in terms of their understanding of God. Quietist Friends saw the world divided between the natural, which they inhabited, and the supernatural, where God resided. The self, which they tried to annihilate, and the worldly, which they tried to avoid, were the barriers between heaven and earth. They lived in fear of their own emotions and of God. Two hundred years later, we find these writers maintaining a dualistic Quietistic theology but one in which God is faced and God's challenges and tricks are welcomed. Celebration and optimism seem to frame these Friends' desires to be faithful. I am refreshed both by the clarity with which God is perceived and the joy with which the accompanied life is faced. If God is a Trickster, this volume celebrates that fact.

❁

Whether you share any of these theological inclinations or even agree with them, I hope you find this book instructive and interesting. I have had a profound sense of privilege working with this group of committed authors and I wish to express my thanks to them all, and to all those who supported them in their writing. I want to thank Rebecca Kratz Mays, Peter Bien and Rachel Howell who were so encouraging of the project, the writers who decided not to contribute, two after months of discernment, and Pam Lunn who helped with software translation as the pieces came in. Thank you.

References
Bledstein, A.J. 'Binder, Trickster, Heel and Hairy-Man: rereading Genesis 27 as a trickster tale told by a woman'. In Brenner, A., ed.,

A Feminist Companion to Genesis. Sheffield: Sheffield Academic Press, 1993: 282-95.

Britain Yearly Meeting of the Religious Society of Friends. *Quaker Faith and Practice: the book of Christian discipline of the Yearly Meeting of Friends (Quakers) in Britain*. London: Britain Yearly Meeting, 1995.

Damiano, K. *On Earth as it is in Heaven: Eighteenth century Quakerism as Realised Eschatology*. PhD thesis. Union of Experimenting Colleges and Universities, 1988.

Dandelion, P. *A Sociological Analysis of the Theology of Quakers: the silent revolution*. Lampeter: Edwin Mellen, 1996.

Hyde, L. *Trickster Makes this World*. New York: Farrar, Straus & Giroux, 1998.

Kazantzakis, N. *The Last Temptation of Christ*, trans. Bien, P. London: Faber, 1987.

Niditch, S. *Underdogs and Tricksters: a prelude to Biblical Folklore*. San Francisco: Harper & Row, 1987.

Radin, P. *The Trickster: A Study in American Indian Mythology*. New York: Schocken Books, 1973.

Richter, P., and Francis, L. *Gone but not Forgotten: church leaving and returning*. London: Darton, Longman & Todd, 1998.

Samuels, A. *The Political Psyche*. London: Routledge, 1993.

Note: all Biblical quotations in the book are from NRSV except where stated.

an excerpt from
Quakerism and the Tricky Way of Wisdom

Chuck Fager
An Introduction to 'Wisdom'

In the early 1830s, a young man went to sea, hoping to make his fortune. A Presbyterian by birth, he read his Bible each night in his shipboard hammock, and he was haunted by a verse in the fourth chapter of Proverbs: 'Wisdom is the principal thing: Therefore, get wisdom: and with all thy getting, get understanding.' Wealth, the youth piously decided, was nothing without this seasoning of wisdom. But where was such a combination to be found?

Presently his ship sailed into the harbor of Nantucket Island. Nantucket was then a wealthy and vibrant community, built and largely populated by members of the Religious Society of Friends.

As he walked the bustling, cobbled streets of Nantucket town, observing the fine grey shingled houses and the plain but prosperous inhabitants, another verse from Proverbs came to him. It was something about, 'I am Wisdom, and in my right hand is riches and honor.'

The more he saw of Nantucketers, the more he felt sure that here was a group that genuinely understood and knew how to apply this kind of Wisdom.

When he turned down one street, which was known then as

'Petticoat Row', he saw a succession of neat, prosperous-looking shops and stores. Almost all were operated by Quaker businesswomen. The sailor was so impressed with this commercial tableau that he impulsively entered one of the shops, a kind of grocery store. He walked up to the counter and said to the plain-dressed woman behind it, 'Madam, I want to know why you Nantucket Quakers seem so wise in the ways of the world.'

The Quaker woman said to him, naturally very humbly, 'Well, of course, it's mainly because we follow the Inward Light. But,' she added, 'it's also because we eat a special kind of fish, the Wisdom Fish.'

'Wisdom Fish?' the sailor exclaimed. 'What's that? Where could I get some?'

'Friend,' the Quaker shopkeeper said, 'thee is in luck. I just happen to have one here, which I can sell thee for only twenty dollars.'

Twenty dollars was a lot of money in those days, but the sailor didn't hesitate. He pulled out his purse, handed over the money, and she gave him a carefully wrapped parcel, which he carried out of the shop with an excited smile on his face.

He returned a few minutes later, however, looking puzzled and a bit disturbed. 'Excuse me, madam,' he said, laying the half-opened package on the counter. 'This is nothing but a piece of ordinary dried codfish.'

Under her modest white bonnet, the Quaker shopkeeper raised one eyebrow. 'Friend,' she said quietly, 'thee is getting wiser already.'

❂

I once worked on a Congressional staff, and this brought me close to a lot of people who were very successful in their fields. Yet anyone who has watched Congress closely will have noticed what I noticed, that many of them lead hard and often frustrating lives. Just how frustrating was shown strikingly in the election year of 1992, when a huge number of them simply threw up their hands and said, 'So What? What's the point? Let me out of here.' There have been similar rushes to retirement in several succeeding years. The same reaction is found among many of us who are less famous and outwardly successful. Take me: when this was first written, in the autumn of 1992, I was earning more than I ever have, and yet I had the urge at least every week to dump it all, move somewhere else and do something else. (All of which, in fact, I have since done.)

And when you get to the 'So what?' part of life, at whatever age and whatever circumstance, whether you know it or not, you are looking for Wisdom.

And 'where,' to quote an earlier seeker, 'is Wisdom to be found?' (Job 28: 12).

Looking to the source

I'm not sure when I realized that the toughest questions in my life all pointed me toward a quest for Wisdom. Nor can I pinpoint when this seeking turned me in the direction of the Bible. Others may find it in different sources; but this is the way I went.

If the date of this turn is hazy, though, the reason is not: I realized that the 'So what?' question had been asked more urgently, wrestled with more memorably and expressed more tellingly than I ever could, in a single phrase from a small book that's more than two thousand years old.

This phrase is one that is, or should be, familiar to us all:

'Vanity of vanities,' saith the Preacher, 'all is vanity and a striving after wind.'

For many of us, a time comes when reading a verse such as this, in the first short chapter of the brief book of Ecclesiastes, is like having something reach out and grab you by the throat. At least that was true for me.

And if the first chapter doesn't do it, the third chapter will:

To everything there is a season, and a time to every purpose under heaven. A time to be born, and a time to die ... (Ecc. 3: 1-2)

How memorable is this text? Well, if it is any measure, I can't think of any other biblical passage that has been the basis of a Top-40 folk-rock hit song.

In any case, beginning a few years back, I was drawn, like an iron filing to a magnet, toward what are called the Wisdom books in the Bible. These books are principally Proverbs, Ecclesiastes, and Job, plus two books found in Catholic Bibles, The Wisdom of Solomon, and Ecclesiasticus, or Sirach. There are Wisdom passages in many other biblical books, but these five will take up most of our attention here.

Part of what drew me to the biblical treasury of Wisdom was simple theology: I believe the Bible has important things to say about what matters in life. And it has been my experience in Bible study that this is indeed the case.

But there was another aspect to this attraction as well, and it had to do with a word that has been very important in the history of the Bible, namely 'revelation'. The Bible has traditionally been presented to Jews and Christians as being in some way a deposit of the self-disclosure of the Divine – as revelation.

The term revelation is usually associated with extraordinary and dramatic events: the parting of the Red Sea; a heavenly voice speaking to Saul on the road to Damascus; phenomenal cures, like Jesus and the woman with an issue of blood; prediction, as when the prophet Jeremiah pronounced the coming doom of Jerusalem; or visions, as of wheels within wheels for Ezekiel; and dreams calling Joseph to flee with Mary and the child to Egypt. Much of the Bible is built around such extraordinary events.

The Wisdom books convey their message without any such marvels. Here by and large we find texts dealing with the most mundane and common of experiences: marriage and family life; farming, business, bureaucracy and government; wealth and poverty. And instead of miracles, or thunderous divine commandments, here we see a process of experience being reflected upon and the results expressed concisely and tellingly.

Furthermore, if there is much talk of kings here, there is as much material drawn from the everyday, even the seemingly inconsequential. In the 30th chapter of Proverbs, for instance, verses 24 through 28 draw our attention to, respectively, ants, badgers, grasshoppers, and lizards. There is not an angel, a burning bush, or a miracle cure anywhere in sight.

The origins of the Wisdom books, like those of most parts of the Hebrew scriptures, are obscure, and there are various theories. But we are not going to dwell on them or try to sort them out. The most important thing about these books, for my purposes, is that these texts are offered to us as a part of the Bible, as part of this deposit of revelation, without explanation or apology.

After reading and reflecting on them, I became persuaded that part of the message of their inclusion in the canon was that revelation can occur, not only through extraordinary and supernatural events, but also – and perhaps most often, even typically, through the ordinary and familiar – if we but understand how to see it.

Thus part of the message of the biblical Wisdom books is that everyday life can be a medium of revelation. That is to say, it too is an arena in and through which the divine discloses itself.

Tricky biblical wisdom

Furthermore, I hadn't gotten very far in this study when I saw, in steadily increasing detail, how consistent its message is with the theme of this book, of God as 'Trickster'. Not that the term explicitly occurs there. But whereas in Proverbs we are repeatedly promised that wise and virtuous living will be graced with both God's approval and worldly success, this confidence is sharply challenged elsewhere, especially in such books as Job, Ecclesiastes, and even the Book of Jonah, which is usually thought of as a 'prophetic' rather than a 'wisdom' text, we find repeatedly the motif of God acting in human affairs in ways that are unpredictable and, from the human perspective at least, capricious or indeed, tricky.

Listen, for example, to Koheleth, the Preacher of Ecclesiastes, summing up his observations of life, in 9: 11, one of those verses which the King James Version (KJV) expresses the best:

> I returned, and saw under the sun, that the race is not to the swift, nor the battle to the strong, neither yet bread to the wise, nor yet riches to men of understanding, nor yet favor to men of skill; but time and chance happeneth to them all (Ecc. 9: 11, KJV).

Or, as the Today's English Version (TEV) more frankly puts the conclusion: 'Bad luck happens to everyone.'

But bad luck was not the worst of what Koheleth saw 'under the sun'. Consider 8: 11-14, which the TEV renders most tellingly:

> Why do people commit crimes so readily? Because crime is not punished quickly enough. A sinner may commit a hundred crimes and still live. Oh yes, I know what they say: 'If you obey God, everything will be all right, but it will not go well for the wicked. Their life is like a shadow and they will die young, because they do not obey God.' But this is nonsense. Look at what happens in the world: sometimes righteous men get the punishment of the wicked, and wicked men get the reward of the righteous. I say it is useless (Ecc. 8: 11-14, TEV).

This is an extraordinary passage, and here I think the TEV serves us far better than most other translations, because it highlights the confrontational character of Ecclesiastes. He is not, in my view, simply offering some friendly constructive criticism to the optimism of other strains of Wisdom writing, such as much of Proverbs, with its innumerable promises of assured prosperity for the righteous and trouble for sinners.

No, Koheleth is going for the jugular; he even takes on theology, and the sages who expounded it, a few verses further on. Again the TEV does the most justice to his radicalism:

Whenever I tried to become wise and learn what goes on in the world, I realized that you could stay awake night and day and never be able to understand what God is doing. However hard you try, you will never find out. Wise men may claim to know, but they don't (Ecc. 8: 16-17, TEV).

Astonishingly, in Ecclesiastes we have an all-out, fundamental challenge to the view of life, and Wisdom, presented in Proverbs, the book immediately preceding it. Nor is it a polite debate; as the TEV's renderings show, it is more like a brawl. You could sum up much of this book in the words of a vulgar slogan I've seen on more than a few bumpers: 'Life's a bitch and then you die.'

This challenge to the assured confidence of Proverbs is deepened by the text that many Bible students consider to be the crown of the Hebrew scriptures, if not the entire Bible, the Book of Job.

You know the story: Job is rich and righteous, but Satan talks God into making a wager on Job's steadfastness if he's subjected to pointless and unjust suffering. So Job's family is killed and he ends up covered with boils and sitting on a manure pile. And as if that's not bad enough, Job is then subjected to a series of sermons from four well-meaning friends, who harangue him endlessly with the Proverbs notion of the good always winning out. This is surely Divine Trickery at its most vulgar and unappealing.

But Job, to his credit, will have none of this; and in Chapter 13, he denounces, not only these false comforters, but the very 'revelation' they are so devotedly, if mindlessly, reiterating:

> Everything you say, I have heard before. I understand it all; I know as much as you do. ... But my dispute is with God, not you ... You cover up your ignorance with lies; you are like doctors who can't heal anyone. Say nothing, and someone may think you are wise! (Job 13: 1, 3, 4-5, TEV).

In Chapter 21, Job really lays it on the line. Again it is in the TEV that its pungency really comes through:

> My quarrel is not with mortal men ... Why does God let
> evil men live, let them grow old and prosper? ... God
> does not bring disaster on their homes; they never have
> to live in terror ... On the day God is angry and pun-
> ishes, it is the wicked man who is always spared (Job 21:
> 4, 7, 9, 30, TEV).

So here we find the comforting Wisdom of Proverbs, not merely questioned, but fiercely – and I think, very effectively – under attack. And this confrontation is the second feature of the biblical Wisdom material that I want to highlight.

One reason to highlight this challenge is that, as gloomy as these parts of the Wisdom writings may seem to some, I find them tremendously refreshing, even uplifting. In fact, I'm not sure I could believe that the Bible is really a special, 'revealing' book, if Ecclesiastes and Job weren't in it ...

Forever Fallen?
Trickster and God-Centred Identity

Jane Orion Smith

Trickster is, broadly speaking, a part of my cultural identity as a Canadian. The concept of Trickster has woven into the wider non-Aboriginal culture along with smudging rituals and sweat lodges. Along the road of cultural appropriation, aspects of each have been revised to fit the (mostly white) culture that wishes a self-fulfilling Aboriginal experience that doesn't ask for any corrective behaviour from us, those who have been destructive of authentic First Nations' cultures and peoples for over 500 years.

Trickster is a figure central within Aboriginal cultures of North America (and elsewhere). When we (Quakers) talk about God as a Trickster, we are on dodgy ground for a true understanding of Trickster is beyond almost all of us, for s/he emerges from the centre of cultures and experiences not our own. For me, this is very important to remember.

Non-Aboriginals have a truncated view of the Trickster where he is the 'other' who interrupts and chaotically overturns our lives. Within the Aboriginal frame of reference, though, the Trickster is much more rich and complex, not simply a 'shadow side' of ourselves or a black-humoured 'other' who trips us up in life. Tomson

Highway, renowned Cree playwright, offers his understanding of Trickster in the foreword to one of his plays:

> The dream world of North American Indian mythology is inhabited by the most fantastic creatures, beings and events. Foremost among these beings is the 'Trickster', as pivotal and important a figure in our world as Christ is in the realm of Christian mythology. 'Weesageechak' in Cree, 'Nanabush' in Ojibway, 'Raven' in others, 'Coyote' in still others, this Trickster goes by many names and many guises. In fact, he can assume any guise he chooses. Essentially a comic, clownish sort of character, his role is to teach us about the nature and meaning of existence on the planet Earth; he straddles the consciousness of man and that of God, the Great Spirit (Highway 1989: 12).

Exploring Trickster seems fundamentally linked to the discovery of our identity and purpose within the context of God and humanity. Highway seems to suggest this in putting forth that Trickster is there to teach us essential lessons about living. As I offer this reflection, please make no mistake: what I say here is not the truth of Trickster to Aboriginal peoples except where such friends are speaking for themselves. While I do not think it is wrong to interpret another's mythology through our own lens, explore how we can relate to, learn from and integrate it, I think one has to be clear that that is what one is doing. It is important to put this upfront, otherwise I follow in the path of those who have taken aspects of Aboriginal culture and reinterpreted them, and stolen them, often without even realising their actions and the injustice it does to Aboriginal culture.

This Trickster, the one I will write about, is mine. Informed foremost by my encounters with God and my culture and history, and interpreted through my experience. That said, I also feel this is a wonderful opportunity to explore – and share – some understanding of who and what Trickster is within his/her own context, with particular emphasis on the aspect that reflects the 'shadow side' of ourselves.

In looking at the formation of a God-centred identity formation resulting from experiences of a Trickster-like presence in our lives, I found it helpful to look at Carl Jung's thoughts on Trickster as the 'shadow' archetype, the observations of Paul Radin, (a well-respected white anthropologist) and Tomson Highway. In looking at the 'dark side' of the Trickster, I wanted to also consider several stories wherein I see Trickster within my own cultural framework: as a Quaker – the events surrounding James Nayler's infamous ride into Bristol in 1656 where he and others recreated Jesus' ride into Jerusalem; as a Christian – the trials and tribulations of Job in the Hebrew Scripture; and, as myself – the unexpected and painful experiences that have tried me.

Identity: just who do you think you are?

Since the 1950s, there has been a strong emergence of (mainly European) Canadian literature, music, theatre, and film focused on exploring identity – who are we? How do we/I view and interact with the world? Of what are our/my interior lives composed? How do first-generation Canadians honour their past and present? To some degree, it has been a self-involved, introspective time. As a country in constant evolution (over half of the citizens of the city of Toronto – and growing – were born somewhere outside Canada), our culture is incapable of stasis without the risk of war.

Why do we care about defining who we are anyway? Claiming an identity is a fundamental act of being and becoming. The self-reflective process of 'identity building' is predicated on a sense of self in relation to other. Canadians may not be able to clearly explain who they are – but they know what they are not: American, for example, with its 'melting pot' approach to new immigrants. Liberal/Universalist Quakers, too, identify themselves by what they are not: hireling ministers, sacrament-based, credal, etc. Yet, by identifying our qualities – strengths and weaknesses, 'light' and sin, beliefs and boundaries – we can learn awareness and to control some aspects of them while nurturing others and developing a clearer sense of what our 'calls' and gifts are in life. This seems central to becoming God-centred rather than self-centred. Herein is the real challenge in Quaker spiritual identity – to realise our God-given selves without getting stuck in the mired mud of secular self-actualisation, to become a Child of the Light instead of a Child of my Light.

Much of Thomas Merton's writings dwell on our alienation from God as a fundamental confusion of identity – theologically and psychologically – wherein our true self (God-centred, empowered and willed) is overarched by the false self (self-centred, empowered, and willed):

> Although God gave us free will, he did not make us omnipotent. We are capable of becoming perfectly godlike, in all truth, by freely receiving from God the gifts of Light and love, of freedom in Christ, the incarnate Logos. Insofar as we are implicitly convinced that we ought to be omnipotent of ourselves, we usurp a god likeness that is not ours. In our desire to be 'as gods', we seek a relative omnipotence: the power to have everything we want, to enjoy everything we desire, to demand that all our wishes be satisfied and that our will should never be frustrated or opposed. It is the need to have everyone else bow to our judgment and accept our declarations as law. It is the insatiable thirst for recognition of the excellence we so desperately need to find in ourselves to avoid despair. This claim to omnipotence, our deepest secret and our inmost shame, is in fact the source of all our sorrows, all our unhappiness, all our dissatisfactions, all our mistakes and deceptions. It is a radical falsity (Merton 1978: 14-15).

And for those who find themselves the doormat instead of the shoe, let me offer the well-circulated words of Marianne Williamson which have become the banner of the New Age:

> Our deepest fear is not that we are inadequate. Our deepest fear is that we are powerful beyond measure. It is our light, not our darkness, that most frightens us. We ask ourselves, who am I to be brilliant, gorgeous, talented and fabulous? Actually, who are you not to be? You are a child of God. Your playing small does not serve the world. There's nothing enlightened about shrinking so that other people won't feel insecure around you. We are all meant to shine, as children do. We were born to make manifest the glory of God that is within us. It's not just in some of us; it's in everyone. And as we let our own light shine, we unconsciously give other people permission to do the same. As we're liberated from our own fear, our presence automatically liberates others (Williamson 1992: 165).

Be it over- or under-recognition of all that we are, there is one common thread – self-centredness. Whether we are stepping on others or ourselves, we put our focus on our self rather than listening for God's trumpet call:

> But now thus says the Lord, he who created you, O Jacob, he who formed you, O Israel: do not fear, for I have redeemed you; I have called you by name; you are mine. When you pass through the waters, I will be with you ... you are my witnesses, says the Lord, and my servant whom I have chosen so that you may know and believe me and understand that I am he. Before me no god was formed, nor shall there be any after me (Isa. 43: 1-2, 10).

In the Christian scheme of identity, 'whoever does not take up the cross and follow me [Jesus Christ] is not worthy of me. Those who find their life shall lose it, and those who lose their life for my sake will find it' (Matt. 10: 38-39). Thomas Merton interprets this as:

> In order to become myself, I must cease to be what I
> always thought I wanted to be (or what others told me I
> was) and in order to find myself, I must go out of myself,
> and in order to live, I have to die (Merton 1972: 47).

The quest for the true self, the God-led self, is one of paradox – dying to the self in order to live through God – and full of opportunities for the Tempter to get the better of us (and, dare I say, the Trickster to teach us). Even Paul, who received the Spirit of Christ, was not immune:

> I do not understand my own behaviour; I do not act as
> I mean to, but I do things that I hate ... for though the
> will to do what is good is in me, the power to do it is
> not: the good thing I want to do, I never do; the evil thing
> which I do not want – that is what I do (Rom. 7: 15, 18b-19).

Trickster: an anthropological perspective

Trickster, meaning the 'cunning one', is the best known player in the mythologies of North American Aboriginal cultures. This outrageous character is familiar across many continents and cultures; as an archetype, s/he is woven into the fabric of what it is to be human. According to anthropologist Paul Radin, in North American Aboriginal cultures:

> Trickster is at one and the same time creator and
> destroyer, giver and negator, he who dupes others and
> who is always duped himself. He wills nothing con-
> sciously. At all times he is constrained to behave as he
> does from impulses over which he has no control. He
> knows neither good nor evil yet is responsible for both.
> He possesses no values, moral or social, is at the mercy
> of his passions and appetites, yet through his actions, all
> values come into being (Radin 1973: xxiii).

This definition resonates with Highway's understanding and one can see aspects of Trickster that might align with Merton's false self and Paul's inner demon. Trickster is, after all, a 'shape shifter', possessing no well-defined, fixed form, often appearing as an animal or human (male or female).

My own culture has co-opted Trickster to refer to an 'other' – fate or God – which has outwitted us or turned our lives upside down in some way. In looking at the Trickster who causes pain and suffering, usually unwittingly, remember that this is a fraction of who s/he is. Understanding Trickster as an 'other' enables us to avoid truths about ourselves and the complexity and mystery of God. It stands in the way of fuller union with God and seeing Trickster as a catalyst for growth, rather than an antagonist. As psychologist Carl Jung notes, we 'never suspect that (our) own hidden and apparently harmless shadow has qualities whose danger exceeds his wildest dreams' (Radin 1973: 206).

In Aboriginal cultures, the Trickster is God-like with supernatural abilities. Says a Winnebago Sioux elder, 'Men [sic] do not understand him ... he does not belong in the world of man but to a much older world' (Radin 1973: 147). Though the Trickster is beyond the human world, he speaks to and reflects it. This continues to this day, as writers like Tomson Highway re-create stories of Trickster that are relative to contemporary Aboriginal peoples, most of whom in Canada live in an urban context and are still contending with the impacts of assimilation and colonisation. This is important work: even with the systematic endeavours to strip Aboriginal peoples of their culture 'trickster did not leave with the white man ... without him, the core of indian culture would be lost' (Highway 1989: 13).

Historically, the Trickster myth cycle of the Winnebago documents the chaotic (and cruel) adventures of Wakdjunkaga ('the tricky one'). The Trickster, as we will see in the myth cycle, is not a static figure stuck in one stage of development – like Paul, he moves from self-centred to God-centred (1 Cor. 13: 11).

The cycle begins with Trickster as a chief who breaks with society by violating cultural taboos going on the warpath alone and to live in the natural world, where he is understood. In the characteristically dark humour that trails Trickster, we find his self-awareness and orientation short-sighted, perhaps child-like, as he swims into the ocean to inquire where the shore is, gets angry and burns his anus then eats his intestines, breaks rules that result in others' deaths, tricks others and is tricked, eats mothers and children to satiate his hunger. The list goes on. Morality and ethics are subsumed by his desire as he creates disorder and chaos. In this cycle, we see his impulse-driven lifestyle (particularly the sexual), is 'completely unanchored' (Radin 1973: 134) and makes him 'a fool' (Radin 1973: 135), a figure who often inflicts pain on himself and others through his lack of consciousness. He imitates others only to trip himself up and, yet, through his adventures, full of pitfalls, he becomes aware of self and world and, ultimately, models the 'good citizen' of society.

After a long time in the village, doing what society expects of him, however, Trickster is chomping at the bit again. A Winnebago elder relates the story:

> One day he said, 'Well, this is about as long as I will stay here. I have been here a long time. Now I am going to go around the earth and visit different people for my children are all grown up. I was not created for what I am doing here.'
>
> Then he went around the earth. He started at the end of the Mississippi river and went down to the stream. The Mississippi is a spirit-village and the river is its main road. He knew that the river was going to be inhabited by Indians and that is why he travelled down it. Whatever he thought might be a hindrance to the Indians he changed. He suddenly recollected the purpose for which he had been sent to the earth by Earthmaker. That is why he removed all these obstacles along the river (Radin 1973: 52).

In reading this text, it is important to factor in another myth featuring Wakdjunkaga, the most sacred *Origin Myth of the Medicine Rite*, where Trickster's purpose is originally noted:

> After Earthmaker created the universe and all its inhabitants, animal and human, he discovers that evil beings are about to exterminate man. In order to help them, he sends Wakdjunkaga, the first being comparable to man he had created, down to earth ... In the *Origin Myth of the Medicine Rite* Wakdjunkaga is described as completely failing. Not even Earthmaker could completely 'rehabilitate' him ... As the myth phrases it, 'Every variety of small evil animals began to play pranks on him and plague him and finally he sat himself down and admitted to himself that he was incapable of doing anything' (Radin 1973: 145).

Originally, Trickster was sent to earth to help humans; through his own will, even with Earthmaker's help, he fails and even admits to being 'incapable of doing anything'. As we see in the later Trickster myth cycle, he understands his purpose is in relation to Earthmaker's will, not his own – this is a shift in consciousness that enables him to now help humans by removing hindrances. In the final scene, he prepares a last supper for himself, high on a rock that the Winnebago can still see today, and then he 'left and went first into the ocean and then up to the heavens. Under the world where Earthmaker lives, there is another world just like it and of this world, he, Trickster, is in charge' (Radin 1973: 53). He becomes as a deity, a symbol of procreative powers and of the human relationship to the universe (Radin 1973: 146). Viewed through my Quaker Christian lens, one might say he now possesses the spirit of Christ and is no longer of this world though in it. One critical difference between Christianity and Trickster is that, with Trickster, whatever the bad behaviour, there is no legacy of guilt.

According to Tomson Highway, Trickster's role 'is to teach us about the nature and meaning of existence on the planet Earth' (Highway 1989: 12). Teaching (and learning) can take many forms – sometimes it is gentle and kind, other times it is a kick in the pants (or worse). Tricksters are here to tell stories from which people/communities learn. While Trickster can inflict cruelty to meet his needs, to imitate others, to cheat and be cheated, to torment and be tormented, to make foolish decisions because of his base desires, s/he can also show compassion, lend a hand, and be a guide. In short, Trickster is composed of the full gamut of who and how we can be in the world. Much like us. Trickster makes choices, sometimes the 'wrong' or stupid choices, but there is always a lesson. He embodies a paradox of identities – tormented/tormentor, winner/loser, cunning/stupid, cheater/cheated, saviour/sinner – that point to a Truth that all is in relation to each other. In viewing the hard-edged shadow side of his ways, we have all met Tricksters.

Trickster in the shadows: a Jungian perspective

To further unpack Trickster within my own socio-cultural frames of reference, Carl G. Jung interprets her/him as 'a "collective personification", a product of a group of individuals and is thus welcomed as something known by other individuals' (Radin 1973: 201). Contemplating the stories and myths that are a part of our culture(s) is a way of exploring (and affirming) our own experience. Stories connect us into a lineage of shared experience that can be an empowering force within identity formation and validation. I exist outside the 'mainstream' when one looks at the 'identity mosaic' that my frames of reference combine to form: Quaker, Christian, woman, Canadian, lesbian, political activist, artist, person with disabilities. The stories that I have read, heard, and told from these various cultures have helped 'name me into existence', and have validated and strengthened me as I seek to walk the path of righteousness that God is laying before me in this particular body and identity. They have also provided me with questions and challenges about God's purpose for me and how that interfaces with identity construction and ego.

Jung configures Trickster as the 'shadow' self (Radin 1973: 201). Our shadows are the epitome of our perceived inferior traits. They never leave us; rather, they wait for a favourable moment to get the better of us. Yet, our shadows can teach us and help us grow too.

Trickster myths can help us look at our 'shadow' self – as individuals and, even more so, as 'nations' (meaning groupings of people with a shared language, land, and culture rather than 'nation states' which are political bodies). In Jung's mind, Trickster myths (which were passed down orally over thousands of years) enabled the listeners to detach and confront, look back and reflect on an earlier state of self (pre-consciousness) (Radin 1973: 202). If Trickster truly is a 'collective personification', then it would be understood that this earlier state of self is a shared stage of identity for all, individually and as the nation (collectivity).

The atrocious things that Trickster can do seem to spring forth from a state of unconsciousness and unrelatedness. As such, awareness of this 'shadow' self, Jung contends, is of particular value as it prevents the dangerous repression of this inherent nature (Radin 1973: 203). Darkness and evil 'have merely withdrawn into the unconscious so long as all is well with the conscious' which can free itself from the 'fascination with evil' and no longer live by it compulsively (Radin 1973: 206). (Trickster is not inherently evil, though, he is better characterised as a 'party animal' out for a good time who sometimes has things go awry.)

Jung's thoughts on freedom from evil (the outward ways of the shadow self) link to Paul's – and early Friends' – assertion that we can all be set free from sin (separation from God) if we live by faith:

> Live by the Spirit, I say and do not gratify the desires of the flesh ... if you are led by the Spirit you are not subject to the law ... And those who belong to Christ Jesus have crucified the flesh with all its passions and desires (Gal. 5: 16, 18, 24).

One is released from the law by living completely by the Spirit (faith). In this state, one will not sin. Whether or not this is fully possible for frail vessels like us is arguable. Yet, as Christians and Quakers, we believe that there is a state beyond the one parametered by social and religious laws; it is the state of Adam (and Eve) before 'the Fall', the state, and new identity, that George Fox and many early Friends came into 'up in spirit through the flaming sword' (Nickalls 1986: 27) which protected the way back into Eden. All creation smelled new, Fox asserted, and one was now sinless (no longer separated from God) and with knowledge (consciousness) and, thus, would not re-enter the fallen identity of Adam, the innocent and 'unconscious'.

As we have seen through Paul's experience, and will see in that of George Fox and James Nayler, outwitting Trickster when he is in 'shadow mode' is more difficult than the faith of men (or women); it really takes the faith of Christ.

Snared by Trickster: the fall of George Fox and James Nayler

In order to explore Trickster in the experience of George Fox and James Nayler, let me briefly tell the tale. In the earlier years of the Quaker movement, James Nayler and George Fox were the most gifted and recognised leaders. By 1656, the Quakers were enjoying immense popularity in London, where Nayler was leading the ministry; by summer, a small group of ardent admirers coalesced around him (Bittle 1986: 84). Conflicts arose amongst Nayler and co-leaders Francis Howgill and Edward Burrough returning from a trip to Ireland, particularly over the issue of authority.

Meanwhile, George Fox had been arrested and jailed in January in Launceston Castle, Cornwall, 'a nasty stinking place', where he remained until September (Bittle 1986: 87, Damrosch 1996: 115). Living in squalid conditions (in contrast to Nayler who was circulating amongst the London posh set), Fox was unable to assess the situation in London first hand. Fox was concerned but harboured no animosity towards Nayler nor was convinced that his followers were, in substance, wrong (Bittle 1986: 90). Rumours about Nayler, including sexual impropriety, circulated and, to add to things, the two leaders had differences of opinion on matters of Quaker practice (Bittle 1986: 91). Letters from Howgill, Burrough, and others arrived at Fox's cell: disruptions of all sorts were occurring in London. Nayler and his cohort were in conflict over the eldering of the converts (Bittle 1986: 94). Fox was quite clear on discipline and was sending steady dicta to Nayler. Increasingly, he perceived a challenge to his leadership. Nayler was to submit to Fox's directives, something which Fox, Margaret Fell, and others now impressed upon Nayler.

There being no appointed leader of the movement, this must have come as a shock to James Nayler. After all, wasn't human autocracy exactly what Friends sought to displace? There was one authority, Christ. A difficulty with this theology, however, was interpretation: if there were varied perspectives on Truth, who had the 'right' one? Clearly, George Fox felt he had it. As did Martha Simmonds, one of Nayler's 'enthusiasts'. James Nayler challenged Fox by refusing to submit to him yet seemed bedevilled in questioning Simmonds' (and others') view of him as, perhaps, Christ himself.

Both men were suffering from physical exhaustion and persecution. As such, their ability to clearly discern must have been impaired. Fox's encounters with Martha Simmonds convinced him that Nayler had turned coat and was out to set himself up as leader (Bittle 1986: 96). Berated, in turn, by Fox and his fellow ministers, Nayler fell into despondency. Finally, in August, Nayler journeyed to Launceston to meet with Fox but was arrested en route and jailed in Exeter.

In a series of meetings with the now-free Fox, neither man seemed able to hear or answer 'that of God' in the other. Without hearing him out, Fox accused Nayler and his followers of being 'out of the Light'. Insult piled upon injury: Nayler and his followers kept their hats on while Fox prayed (implying his prayers were not Spirit-led); Nayler ignored Fox's salutations when he came to his cell one day, refused to meet him at an appointed inn the next day, and, then, in a meeting on the street, publicly called Fox a liar (Bittle 1986: 98). Nayler felt that Fox had been all too willing to believe unfavourable reports about him. This left him 'in conflict and turmoil over his relations with Fox' (*Ibid.*).

The final meeting and breach on the next day saw Fox berating Nayler at length, particularly for calling him a liar in public. Nayler 'wept and professed a great love and ... offered George an apple' which he refused (Bittle 1986: 99). With Fox's hand in his, Nayler asked if he might kiss him and, unwilling to bow down to enable this act, 'George gave him his hand to kiss but he would not, and then George said unto him, "It is my foot" (and offered him his boot to kiss)' (Bittle 1986: 99; Fox [1952] 1986: 269). Fox later said that 'the Lord God moved me to slight him' and that Nayler's greatest burden was 'resisting the power of God in me' (Fox [1952] 1986: 269). It seems Fox believed that the Truth was his! 'In a movement which placed so much stress on the basic equality of the individual ... it is difficult to imagine any action on Fox's part which would have wounded Nayler as deeply' (Bittle 1986: 99).

After leaving Exeter, Fox travelled and informed Friends that Nayler and his followers were 'rebellious' and accused Nayler of 'prejudice and jealousy' (Bittle 1986: 100). Conflict increased with Nayler indecisive as to his role in the leadership and disillusioned, as his view of 'Fox as the personification of Quaker ideals had been shattered' (Bittle 1986: 102).

Nayler and his followers decided to enact a 'sign' that would bear witness to the come and coming of Christ within to a war-ravaged England. Some speculate it was a sign designed to set up Nayler as the true leader of the Quaker movement. On October 24, a rag tag group of men and women led a worn James Nayler into Bristol in a recreation of Christ's entry into Jerusalem.

Bristol Friends refused them; they were arrested and imprisoned. Nayler was subsequently sent to London and tried by a Parliament now hostile to the radical religious counterculture that Quakers represented. Abandoned by almost all Friends, Nayler testified in his defence that he was not Christ but witnessed to Christ within him. Although former army comrades appeared and spoke in his favour, Fox, Nayler's longtime friend and comrade, did not. In two letters to Parliament, George Fox, arrested for blasphemy on several occasions himself, spoke to the incarnational doctrine of Friends and, while not condemning Nayler, made it clear that if

> ... blasphemy it was, so should it be punished. To his credit, Fox pushed Parliament to consider the possible authenticity of Nayler's sign (Gwyn 1995: 168-9).

On December 17, Parliament resolved that Nayler was guilty; an excessively brutal litany of punishments was carried out (see Bittle 1986: 132). The movement was forever changed by these events, and the ushering in of the kingdom of God on earth delayed once more. George Fox and the early Friends now turned to the establishment of a structure to test leadings, conduct business and rein in people 'out of the Light'.

Sorting through the carnage ...

Nayler and Fox both fell prey to pranks of Trickster and their personal shadow in 1656. While adulations such as 'thy name is no longer James but Jesus' may have turned Nayler's head (it certainly confused and distressed him), Fox expected that all should be 'of George' – at least in terms of authority over the movement. The letters and meetings (rife with rumours, misunderstandings, power conflicts, ego, and rebuffs) resulted in a near fracturing of the movement. Their friendship and joint ministry in ruins, and no 'coolness of thought' in sight, all barrelled towards further disaster in true Trickster form in the days following Exeter.

Trickster saw a good time of mischief to be had and jumped for it: all sorts of scenarios arose wherein the offerings of personal desire (and power) were high. Both George and James followed the lures and bit the bait. No one emerged looking 'good'; all became victims of their own actions and egos. In their struggle, Nayler and Fox both fell from grace, taking Friends with them.

In part, the persecutions of Friends which intensified after Nayler's ride, must be laid at George Fox's feet. Even with recognising Nayler's part and Parliament's vigilant desire to 'make him example' to rein in radical religious movements like the Quakers, Fox's actions have outfoxed scrutiny as a causal factor that intensified the effects of the 'Bristol incident'. Fox's instruction to Friends to refuse Nayler when he arrived in Bristol and to effectively disown him when he was tried by Parliament have not been considered as being beyond necessary means to prevent the further destruction of the movement. George Fox's letter to the Parliament committing Nayler to their brutal judgment was a compassionless act, comparable, in Quaker history, to the betrayal of Christ. Fox, of all, knew well what became of Jesus after sign of the coming of the kingdom; 'crucifixion' was in the air and Fox, instead of being faithful, sold the lamb to slaughter through fear and negligence if not overt malice.

Friends seem undisturbed to have a 'crucified' and well-buried James Nayler; we have ignored the lessons of Trickster who played havoc with him and George Fox. Did Fox, in his efforts to save the movement, and assert his leadership, let *his* will take the reins instead of listening for God's leadings? Did Nayler 'outrun his Guide' to the extreme Fox insinuated? Was there a grain of truth in his, and his followers', criticisms of Fox's claim of authority over the movement? Was Nayler's ride an act of wilful self-aggrandisement or a powerful witness to the come and coming Christ – or both? What if Nayler had appropriately eldered his followers so that the 'message' was not contaminated by any delusions of him as the Christ? What opportunity may have been missed by Friends if they had rallied around Nayler and challenged the Parliament instead of abandoning him? Did the conflict ignite a desire in Fox to be the unquestioned leader? By falling prey to Trickster cunning, instead of Christly compassion, did Fox's actions post-Bristol make the movement more vulnerable to persecutions, not less?

Cunning and stupidity, as Trickster shows, can go hand in hand.

Perhaps, this was a time when Fox (and Nayler) should have heeded the advice he dispensed in a letter in 1652:

> Friends, whatever ye are addicted to, the tempter will come in that thing; and when he can trouble you, then he gets advantage over you, and then you are gone. Stand still in that which is pure ... that which shows and discovers ... and submit to it, and the other will be hush'd and gone (Britain YM 1995: 20.42).

The Tempter came in the question, 'Who was the leader of the Quakers? Who holds final authority over the flock?' Instead of leaning on the source of our strength and wisdom, Fox exerted his own. Nayler became mired and defensive in his own ego, hurt feelings and understandable alienation from Fox which impaired his ability to straighten things out with God's help.

I have asked myself many questions about how things might have been different regarding this pivotal incident in Friends' history. What if Nayler had faced his own conflicted needs of affirmation and difficulties with managing conflict which seemed evident in London? What if James Nayler had appropriately eldered Simmonds in London (and elsewhere)? What if George Fox had waited to hear Nayler's side of the story before laying accusations and assuming rebellion against him? What if Fox had opened his eyes to the possibilities of a movement with several leaders (as there were) with many strengths and gifts to bear? What if Fox and Nayler had been able to come together with an assumption of brotherhood (rather than adversarially) and met in a worshipfulness where they could truly hear each other? And even if none of this was possible, what if, instead of cutting off Nayler, a longtime faithful minister of the Truth, Fox had rallied the Quaker forces around him with a vengeance as he stood trial in Westminster? What an opportunity was possibly missed! For the Quaker Truth to go head-to-head with the religions invested in the Parliament – for a climactic 'Lamb's Warre' battle to be fought in the centre of political power, one that might have put England one step closer to the just Kingdom they sought! Would not the Trickster, seeking self preservation, gratification, and authority, have been thwarted and a higher Will served?

We will never know, but it is enticing to ponder ...

With this, so it seems, came the end of living by faith alone. In late 1656, a letter from the Elders of Balby was sent out to Friends everywhere, prescribing conduct and eldership. The famous postscript of the letter noting that 'these things we do not lay upon you as a rule or a form to walk by' but so that all may be guided in the Light (Britain YM 1995: 1.01) only applied to the advices and queries included in the missive. Fox and his faithful then set about the task of galvanising the movement under his leadership and organising the scattered meetings of Friends into a structure, that endures to this day, which would enable the testing of leadings, the oversight of business, the support of those suffering and serving in the name of Friends, and the eldering of those in need of it. So who can say nothing good came out of all this mess – even if we did miss bringing about the kingdom of God?

Even though there was terrible personal and collective fallout from these events, there were lessons learned. Friends realised we must test leadings and that, if we were to survive as a people, we had to have a structure and appropriate discipline. Thus, even through the shadow side operations of Trickster, good can come forth.

Can God be a Trickster?

Much evil and ill will that befalls people and creation each day can be explained away by the 'shadow' side of humanity – violence of all stripes, greed, ignorance, and oppression. Still, there is much that befalls us that has no human origin: disease, drought, natural disasters, accidents, and death itself. Whereas the Psalmists call on God to destroy the enemies that torment them, Job is subject to disease and many misfortunes that are beyond human contrivance. Does God permit evil and punishment to bear on the innocent and faithful? Can God be a Trickster in this fashion?

One story that asserts God as Trickster in this way is that of Job. While there is not space for a full exploration of Job, it is useful to, at least as an aside, address this issue of God as Trickster. Job is a pious, upstanding and successful man. This is visible to all and pleases God:

> The Lord said to Satan, 'Have you considered my servant Job? There is no one like him on earth, a blameless and upright man who fears God and turns away from evil' (Job 1: 8).

Not all that impressed, Satan responds:

> 'Does Job fear God for nothing? Have you not put a fence around him and his house and all that he has, on every side? You have blessed the work of his hands ... But stretch out your hand now, and touch all that he has, and he will curse you to your face' (Job 1: 10-11).

Not to be one-upped by Satan's cynicism in humanity, God makes a deal with the Devil:

> 'Very well, all that he has is in your power; only do not stretch out your hand against him!' (Job 1: 12).

Well, this sounds as adventurous as the lions and the Christians in Rome. Satan throws fireball after fireball of tragedy and strife against Job. As his family is killed, his wealth eradicated and his body plagued with illness, Job remains faithful. It was customary to believe, at the time, that such misfortune came from one's own separation from God, sinfulness, yet Job professed (and exhibited) no sin. Overwhelmed by his sufferings and the poor comfort of his 'friends', Job seeks to make sense of it himself. Yet, is there any sense that a human can make of all this? Finally, God speaks to Job:

> Then the Lord answered Job out of the whirlwind: 'Gird up your loins like a man; I will question you and you declare to me. Will you ever put me in the wrong?

Will you condemn me that you may be justified? Have
you an arm like God, and can you thunder with a voice
like his?' ... Then Job answered the Lord: 'I know that
you can do all things, and that no purpose of yours can
be thwarted. Who is this that hides counsel without
knowledge? Therefore, I have uttered what I did not
understand, things too wonderful for me, which I did
not know' (Job 40: 6-9; 42: 1-3).

Job was tempted to believe that God was a Trickster in his life in
so far as his life was turned upside down. Yet, to be a Trickster means
for God to will nothing consciously himself, to possess 'no values,
moral or social, [to be] at the mercy of his passions and appetites, yet
through his actions, all values come into being' (Radin 1973: xxiii).
God struck an arrangement with Satan, clearly aware of the consequences – why else would he put a restriction on how far Satan could
go in this? An interpretation of God as Trickster also has affinity
with our Quaker Christian understanding of God: the One who
through the Light reveals God's will to us, teaches us good and evil,
and guides those who live by faith. Our experiences in life, even as
we act in faith, can feel full of 'tricks'. Sometimes I can almost see a
sly smile on God's face as I read this story or as I encounter my own
misfortunes for I know – and God and Trickster know – that these
are opportunities for transformation and refinement.

In Job's case, the symbol of faithfulness, he sought to go beyond
pure faith by venturing to make sense of that which is beyond our
comprehension or knowing (and God set him straight!). This is, of
course, a very uncomfortable thought for those of us living in the
'information age', a time when we feel we can know all or, at the
minimum, that all is within our grasp. At the same time, this very
thought makes us vulnerable to self-centredness and aggrandisement
within the commonplace contemporary notion of humans as co-
creators within the universe rather than instruments of God's will.
When we rise above being teachable, tricks await.

Facing Trickster truth in my life

As for myself, I've wanted to believe God was a Trickster many times: growing up with a schizophrenic mother (and all that entailed), having unexplainable illnesses befall me, having partners I loved leave me. All these situations left me battered and confused, even humiliated and destroyed, and believing that God was a Trickster, albeit one who was turning my life upside down in order to draw me closer.

Never was the presence of Trickster so intense and transformative as in my relationships. Through mistakes and misguided notions, I have caused havoc and found myself turned upside down and inside out by the Spirit. Like Trickster, malice was never my intent, but fulfilment of my ego and desires fogged my behaviour. Through my relationships, I have learned how power can be subtly abused when one is not being honest with oneself about one's intentions, needs etc. Over time, I have become a particularly careful friend and partner. I like to think of this as part of my restitution.

In times of brokenness, I realised the profound power of self-forgiveness and of God's love to reawaken and reform me in her image. The love and support of f/Friends was important in this time of change. An important lesson that I have had occasion to use frequently is that good people can do 'bad' things, even evil things, and acknowledging our capacity, like Trickster, for all manner of behaviour is vital to dealing with the 'tough stuff' and being 'community' in its fullest sense.

Asking questions about God as Trickster meant having to consider my own egocentric view of justice and punishment. Most of us view the things that happen to us through the lens of our own will and desires, sense of happiness and achievement. Often these 'lenses' are caught masquerading as God's will. In such moments, are we simply being shown that we are more self-centred than God-centred and, perhaps, even, have outrun our Guide?

Have we come to terms with the realities of an earthly world that, by its nature, destroys and recreates itself? Is my mother's schizophrenia or my illnesses (or bad behaviour) any different, less natural (or purposeful) than the life cycle of the seasons? The glorious autumn leaves, now coming to full, are falling outside my window as I write, filling the air with the sweet smell of death. It's getting cold, and soon the fallow earth, almost devoid of the signs of life, will be covered by a starry, white blanket dazzling in the morning sun. I will await spring, which brings rain and buds of green, new life, and blossoms into the ripeness and bounty of summer. I have found the lessons of the seasons in the fallow and full rhythms of my life.

Is a consideration of good and evil possible in such circumstances or are we being driven by our own desires and self- (or other-) constructed identities? In the beginning, God created the darkness and the light which, in our first symbol of wholeness and unity, made up the first day (Gen. 1: 1-5). There is a time for everything and a season for every activity under the sun (Ecc. 3: 1); this is the natural order. Every season has its gifts (warmth, harvest, water) and its perils (heat waves, cold snaps, droughts). As much as we would all prefer sweetness and light, life, fundamentally, is a balance of paradoxical things.

I have witnessed all aspects of Trickster in (and around) me – even as I have denied and resisted the truth of it, wanting to point my finger at others. As our friend George Fox said:

> And I saw the state of those, both priests and people, who in reading the Scriptures, cry out much against Cain, Esau, and Judas, and other wicked men of former times ... but do not see the nature of Cain, of Esau, of Judas and those others, in themselves. And these they said it was they, they, they, that were the bad people; putting it off from themselves: but when some of these came, with the light and spirit of Truth, to see themselves, then they came to say 'I, I, I, it is I myself that have been the Ishmael and the Esau', etc. For then they came to see the nature of wild Ishmael in themselves ...
> (Nickalls 1986: 30).

I have 'outrun my Guide', misled myself (and others) with regards to what was my will and what was God's will. I have been tripped up, set up, cheated, and tormented and inflicted the same on others, most often through the unconscious self-indulgent movements of Trickster within me. Some days, I think my self-will has resurrected its life from God's crucifying Light more times than a cat has lives. Yet, I know I have come closer to God and that my desire to submit to his will is genuine. Like Paul, I find 'I do not do what I want, but the very thing I hate [follow my own will]' (Rom. 7: 15). And he's right: the power to do it is not in me, it is in Christ, whom I must continually be mindful of and, when I fall, redeemed by.

Becoming bound up by guilt, shame, and alienation from God – sin – is purposeless; to let the Light reveal and release us from it is the path to freedom and Truth. Quakers would be well to consider the usefulness of a 'meeting for confession' and other methods of redemption as it seems, try as we might, we are almost destined to fall again and again, even as we profess (and strive) to live by the Light. We require means for reconciliation to the Light and each other, means that are not privatised as the shared experience has the ability to convince and liberate others, as the early Friends' witness shows.

Moreover, these encounters with Trickster – or experiences we may wish to name as God as a Trickster in our life, Aboriginal definition suspended – are really encounters with transformative energy and opportunity. They are not to be avoided but waded into and divined through. For deep within, under the shadows and darkness is the primordial fire of God within us, seeking to shift and rip open our tectonic plates of resistance, to consume us into its Light so that it might burn through us and radiate its love all the more in the world. Tomson Highway reminds me that 'human existence isn't a struggle for redemption to the Trickster. It's fun, a joyous celebration' (Preston 1990: 36).

God is neither good nor evil and free will is ours. We use it and the ends are ours to determine by our choices.

Conclusion

We are the light and the dark and will experience all manner of each in our lives. This makes us whole, just as the day. As we clamour to find identities rooted in outward forms – our jobs, our relationships, our nations and cultures – we are called to enter into the primal identity, one hinged on a humble relationship with God (Micah 6: 8). If we can find one constant in our lives, perhaps, it is this orientation towards, subjugation to, and identity in God, hard as it may be to maintain. Trickster can throw the clay pot wildly off-centre; only God can re-centre us. Without clarity about our 'shadow' self, and what our sense of identity is predicated on, we are vulnerable. In being centred by (and in) God, I believe that God will hold us in the centre. But it is easy to think we are holding the centre of God and, thus, like Fox and Nayler, we must remain ever-mindful of not outrunning – or falsely becoming – our Guide.

We need not expect the impossible of ourselves; simply believe that all is possible in Christ/Spirit. Jesus set an example of rising above personal identity needs as he prayed in Gethsemane, 'My Father, if it is possible, let this cup pass from me; yet not what I want but what you want' (Matt. 26: 39b). Death on the cross for a Hebrew outwardly signified the ultimate separation from God – the furthest thing from Jesus's truth. Jesus laid aside all outward interpretations, trusting that God's will and truth would be known through the witness of his life, his true self. Would that the early Friends had acted the same after Bristol. Would that we trusted God like that today.

Are we forever fallen? Our whole lives will be lived out in flesh and be prey to its desires and identity:

> As we grow, we develop a mental, inward image of what and who we are until it stands like a great tree in us, blocking the light and impoverishing the soil. This is a false image; it is the false self that we value and worship. It will die eventually, and we must allow it to be destroyed in us if we are not to die with it. When the fire (see Malachi 3: 1-3) comes to burn it up we should rejoice

because we shall be renewed and restored. The fire is feared precisely because people do not want to give up what they see as their identity, their material possessions and the good opinion of others that they connect with their own self-esteem (Langford 1987: 10).

I understand and struggle with that fear, all the while stretching my own self (and personae) to open further and further to the transformative, synthesising fires of the Light. Seeking perfection (translated to me by Woodbrooke tutor Timothy Peat as 'a single-mindedness of the heart') and salvation of Christ is meaningful to me, if what we mean by that is wholeness (from the Latin 'salvo'); we can experience it by living up to our measure of the spiritual Light that illumines us from within. And, then, more will be given to us.

Through the Christ spirit, I feel we are somewhere between the worlds. We can dance with Trickster, embracing, confronting, loving, and transforming experiences. Through our falls, and redemptions, we come to more deeply know a spiritual will which, as James Nayler learned, 'delights to endure all things, in hope to enjoy its own in the end', which 'bears no evil in itself, so it conceives none in thoughts to any other', which 'never rejoiceth but through sufferings; for with the world's joy it is murdered' for it can rejoice 'in God alone' (Britain YM 1995: 19.12). Perhaps, as Jung suggests, 'only out of disaster can the longing for a saviour arise' (Radin 1973: 211).

And through this, one hopes, we can come to live in the Spirit, in true faith, and to learn to distinguish the wisdom from above from that which is from beneath, and to value our encounters with the cunningness of the Trickster as opportunities for God's kingdom to break forth all the more into this one through our conscious, God-centred responses. Thus, may we come further into our True Selves, our real and penultimate identity as Children of the Light, knowing ourselves and acting in the world inwardly from God.

Special thanks to Jennifer Preston Howe, Aboriginal Affairs Program Associate of Canadian Friends Service Committee, who gave me new perspectives on Trickster.

References

Bittle, W. G. *James Nayler: the Quaker Indicted by Parliament*. York: Sessions, 1986.

Britain Yearly Meeting of the Religious Society of Friends. *Quaker Faith & Practice*. London: Britain Yearly Meeting, 1995.

Damrosch, L. *The Sorrows of the Quaker Jesus*. Cambridge, Massachusetts: Harvard University Press, 1996.

Nickalls, J.L., ed. *The Journal of George Fox*. London: London Yearly Meeting of the Religious Society of Friends, 1986. First published Cambridge: Cambridge University Press, 1952.

Gwyn, D. *The Covenant Crucified: Quakers and the Rise of Capitalism*. Wallingford, Pennsylvania: Pendle Hill Publications, 1994.

Highway, T. *Dry Lips Outta Move To Kapuskasing*. Saskatoon, Saskatchewan: Fifth House Publishers, 1989.

Ingle, L.H. *First Among Friends: George Fox and the Creation of Quakerism*. Oxford: Oxford University Press, 1994.

Langford, M. *Making a Fresh Start with George Fox and the Bible*. Gloucester: George Fox Fund, 1987.

Merton, T. *The Silent Life*. New York: Farrar, Straus & Giroux, 1978.

Merton, T. *New Seeds of Contemplation*. New York: New Directions Publishing House, 1972.

Preston, J.C. 'Tomson Highway: Dancing to the Tune of the Trickster'. Unpublished MA thesis, Guelph, Ontario, 1990.

Radin, P. *The Trickster: A Study in American Indian Mythology*. New York: Schocken Books, 1973.

Williamson, M. *A Return to Love*. San Francisco: HarperCollins, 1992.

Other useful sources

Dandelion, B.P., Gwyn, D., and Peat, T. *Heaven on Earth: Quakers and the Second Coming*. Birmingham and Kelso: Woodbrooke College and Curlew Productions, 1998.

Stern, C.E. *Quaker Worship: We Cannot Do It On Our Own*. New Foundation Fellowship, 1995.

A Very Shabby Fellow

Jan Arriens

Towards the end of his life, Bertrand Russell, the celebrated English philosopher and atheist, was asked what he would say if he met God after he died. 'I should say,' replied Russell in his high-pitched voice, 'you're a very shabby fellow, as you did not give us the evidence.'

Russell had a point. God – in the sense of some transcendent reality – is tantalizingly elusive. If we seek to get in touch with those realms, life is a mist or mystery. I sometimes think that if hell is being as far removed from God as possible without losing all sense of contact, then our earthly existence must be hell.

On top of that there are those living in a human hell for whom the notion of God must ring very hollow. What comfort is it to say to someone whose life has been savagely turned upside down by war in Kosovo, Rwanda or the Congo that the ways of God are mysterious but we must keep our faith? What of people who suddenly lose loved ones in a calamity? Or people struck down by debilitating disease while still in the prime of life? Or who lose their home and means of livelihood in a flood or earthquake? This chapter examines how affliction can paradoxically help us transcend our sense of individuality, how we go through life facing two ways at once – the whole and the individual – and how God is essentially a Trickster because we tend to approach God from the vantage point of the individual – especially in this age of individualism.

Job and affliction

Probably the most celebrated example of someone whose faith was tested by affliction was Job in the Old Testament. Job has everything taken away: his loved ones, his possessions and his health. His ultimate faith is not shaken, but he does question the ways of God and laments his very birth. In our secular age, it is common – and understandable – to find people who are moved to deny the existence of any God capable of such wanton caprice, or who curse and rail against God's indifference.

This is more than just the age-old question of how God can be both all-good and all-powerful. Job, it may be remembered, finally has an encounter with God, in which he is forced to admit his total ignorance of the mysteries of life. But it *is* an encounter – the encounter Job has been longing for in his privation. Confronted by the immediacy of such revelation, Job willingly enters into and embraces the Mystery. But what of those who do not have such an experience?

There can be but few people who have not at some point or another had a sense of transcendence, of something greater than themselves of which they form part. Often, it is just a fleeting and indefinable sense, an echo or shadow, prompted perhaps by the splendour of a sunset or the majestic beauty of the sea. These moments are part of the very stuff of life, and people react to and interpret them very differently. Blake sees a world in a grain of sand and heaven in a wild flower; others regard such sensations as no more than heightened sensory inputs.

Mystical experiences

I remember that on the last morning of the World Conference of

Friends held in the Netherlands in 1991, I woke up with a sense of being utterly held by God. I was in tears, trying not to wake those in the bunks beside me, and entered in my diary that this was an experience 'I will never forget'. On rereading my diary some years later, I realized that I *had* forgotten it, in the sense that it had retreated from my conscious memory. On the one hand, I had had an experience which, at the time, I would have adduced as personal evidence of God; but, so tricky is that part of our consciousness that I might some years later have complained, until my memory was jogged by my diary, at the tenuousness of the evidence that 'God' provides us.

Other people, however, have experiences that stay with them and which leave them in no doubt. These are experiences that go beyond words, but which leave the person concerned with a sense of deep inner certainty, and which can sometimes change their lives and beliefs completely. Often the experiences are associated with a sense of unity and the essential benevolence of the universe. There is also a complete conviction that the world is not as we know it, as though a veil had momentarily lifted and we had been vouchsafed a glimpse beyond our normal limits of perception.

Research carried out by bodies such as the Alister Hardy Trust in Britain suggest that such experiences are not uncommon. Indeed, if there are others like me who manage to forget what would otherwise be known as a peak experience, the true figure may be even higher than the research suggests. There is also the extremely intriguing phenomenon of near-death experiences, which medical science is unable satisfactorily to explain.

In my own case, I had an experience ten years ago which far from being tucked away in the recesses of my mind has remained with me vividly ever since. The circumstances are unimportant, except that a difficult decision had been made with a friend. Afterwards we were standing quietly in her hallway when we both had a sense of a cloak descending around us. We did not speak about it at the time, except to note that it had happened, but then quite independently wrote accounts that were almost identical.

The cloak, or embrace, was quite unlike anything I had ever experienced before. Above all it had a quality of utter benevolence and benignness – or, as I have just mistyped it, 'beingness': here was a different dimension, more real than the apparent reality of the day-to-day world we ordinarily inhabit. Time and again I have fallen back on those moments, lasting perhaps 30 seconds, at times of doubt, pain and darkness. They cannot be taken away, and they cannot be explained away. They are realer to me than I am to myself.

When I was at university in Melbourne, I was greatly influenced by the Master of Queen's College, Dr Raynor Johnson. The Master was a highly respected physicist who, in the 1950s and 1960s, wrote a number of authoritative and pioneering works in the field of mysticism and psychical research. As a scientist, he began with the evidence. Unlike many other scientists, however, he did not simply dismiss what he could not explain. Instead, a number of his books begin with remarkable and compelling accounts of personal experiences. To take one example, from *Watcher on the Hills* (1959), a young couple is climbing a hill and the woman is afflicted with asthma:

> We struggled up the hill, and the next thing I noted was that the whole locality was illumined by an extraordinary, bright light. Accompanying the light was the sense of the presence of an irresistible power wholly and utterly benevolent, and as far as I was concerned a feeling of complete happiness and well being quite impossible to describe. After an appreciable interval – I think a few minutes – the light gradually faded and I said to my companion, 'Did you see that?'
>
> But she had not noticed anything unusual, and so the experience was obviously psychical and not physical. However, she turned to me and said, 'My asthma is all gone' – and this disease has never reappeared (Johnson 1959: 49).

The sense of light

The sense of light is a recurrent motif in mystical and also near-death experiences. One of the most extraordinary visitations by light I have come across concerns a prisoner on Death Row in Florida, Michael Lambrix. After he had been there for five years he was served a death warrant, and came within hours of execution. The morning on which his execution had been scheduled, he woke from a dream.

> It was more than just a nightmare – it was an 'out of body' experience. I didn't just dream it, I physically felt it, even the execution. And awoke just as the bright light consumed everything. The immense light I sensed as I was awaking was not a physical, environmental light – as that obviously would have been noticed by the guards who stood watch over me. This light I can only describe as that *sense* of light people experiencing 'near death' experiences describe.
>
> I had reached the point of accepting death, at a depth of the inner self that simply cannot be described. It's like something inside just lets go. And it was through that period of time that I experienced that 'virtual reality' death.
>
> I didn't die, though. But God did, as prior to that throughout my entire life I always felt a personal inter-connection with God, even when I turned my back on Him. But not after that experience. That's why it's so hard to explain in words. It's that sense of His existence that made me believe He really was there. But that sense of the presence died in that nightmare/OBE, and I've never felt it since.
>
> You know, you're the first person I've ever actually told all that to, and I didn't really plan to, it just rolled on out. I can tell you this. There is no experience more intense than death and it's that experience more than anything else that tells me there really is a God. So many

times throughout my life I prayed in times of need. But not on death watch, so I really don't know why that nightmare came about. But I do know what I felt – and what I haven't felt since. I can't explain why everything in my life has brought only pain and loss. But neither can I understand why the consciousness of God 'died' within me when I needed Him the most, when I was totally alone facing my third scheduled execution in one week. But that experience was more 'real' than anything I ever felt in my life. It was so real, I *can't* deny it.

I must also admit that there are times since the 'death' of that former perception of God when I really miss that 'personal' feeling. The way this transformation of my spirituality came about, it allows me to relate to the anguish Jesus felt at the moment of his death – how he cried out 'why hast thou forsaken me', as I think that he too felt that absence and emptiness of the spiritual inner-self. Yet equally so, I truly believe that I did not actually lose anything – but I gained a new and 'more enlightened' perspective of what this thing we call 'God' is, and more importantly, whereas before I could only wonder if there was life after 'death', I am now unequivocally convinced that not only is there 'life' after mortal death – but that we 'lived' before this mortal existence. Our 'personal' God is a reflection of our spiritual selfishness and as long as we want to possess it then we are limited in our growth and perception of collectiveness (Arriens 1997: 223).

Here we are faced by a twofold problem. On the one hand, an experience as profound as this prisoner's can lead us to redefine our whole conception of God away. God is such a trickster that even when we have the evidence, the perceived source can then change. Secondly, experiences of this profundity are rare, they cannot be reproduced in a laboratory, and, at their most profound, they cannot even be put into words.

So God is elusive and, when we do receive some intimation, turns out to be a chameleon or a chimera. For most of us, we do not have the certainty brought by a dialogue such as Job had with God. There is the further problem that the 'evidence' comes from a different realm of consciousness – and cannot therefore be satisfactorily translated into ordinary human communication. Hence we have the poets and music, which enable us to respond to the unspoken rhythms and resonances of life. But more than this, we must ask why this should be so. Why does God hide? Why can we be driven by this shabby fellow to rail like Job? Why, more than that, does the elusiveness of God provide such fertile ground for scientific reductionism and humanism?

Part of the answer – for our view is necessarily partial – goes I believe to the heart of the human condition. Mystical experience in which we receive unbidden intimations of a greater whole is essentially about merging with that whole and losing our sense of self or individuality. If this is so, it means that the perceiver is the chimera, not the God. In the very act of 'seeking' we are bringing to the fore the self that is 'lost' when we merge with the universe. In seeking to identify God we are as it were looking through the wrong end of a telescope. It is the individual that lacks reality, not God.

The elusive individual

The more we look at the individual, the harder to grasp or define it becomes. In physical terms, we are constantly changing: as I type these words, electrical impulses are altering the configuration of my brain. With each passing moment, I am slightly different from the individual noting that moment. I am constantly shedding cells; indeed it is said that every cell in the body is replaced every seven years. Apart from which we cannot even define ourselves in isolation from our surroundings. We are critically dependent on the air entering and leaving our lungs. At what stage is the air we breathe in part of us rather than part of the 'outside' world?

More, we are influenced by outside forces. The presence of one person affects us differently from that of another, even though there may be no physical contact. One person makes us feel joyful and animated, another leaves us uneasy. Or the force may be unseen, as in the case of telepathy. Another's thoughts can enter my realm of consciousness; so, equally, can my apparently private, sealed-off thoughts in fact be shared with others.

Now it is this individual, whom we cannot define and who melts before our very eyes the more we seek to pin it down, which is so concerned to know – or deny – 'God'. In other words, the very concept of God is borne of our illusory sense of separateness and individuality. This is why the mystics have often exclaimed that they are God – a truth they were unable to deny, even though in medieval times it could cost them their lives. So our notion of God is intimately bound up with our sense of individual separateness, and it is in this sense that God died for Mike Lambrix on Death Row.

I have never understood the logic of why God could have a son – the two being mutually exclusive concepts – and further why God would then have that son killed and thereby wipe the slate clean for sinful mankind. But Jesus also talks of being born again, and this dying to the self is a concept central to all the great religions. It is when we die to the self that we join the mystical whole, which we may call God. It is not (I believe!) that God dies for us, but that we die to join God. The 'sin' for which Jesus purportedly died is the original sin of our separateness; that moment in evolution, symbolised by the Garden of Eden, at which humankind became conscious of its own consciousness and found itself facing two ways at once. Sin is the loss of innocence, the birth of individuality. It is this which needs to be sacrificed in order to wipe away the separation and merge again with the whole.

Searching for God

So searching for God is as elusive as the pot of gold at the end of the rainbow. It is not the seeker who will find. We seek something we will never find, to find something we never lost. It is because we are looking through the wrong end of the telescope that such paradox abounds.

This line of thought suggests we are part of a greater whole but apprehend this only dimly because we are obliged to function in the 'real' world as individual entities. It suggests that the 'whole' was always there, but that in the process of evolution we lost our sense of identification with it.

Let me illustrate this by a story told by Felicity Kelcourse at the Fifth World Conference of Friends at Elspeet in the Netherlands in 1991. Felicity spoke early on in the Conference, when we were still unsure whether the divisions between the unprogrammed and programmed traditions – and especially the position of Jesus – would prove bridgeable. At the end of her talk, she related how she had spent one Christmas in hospital after an ectopic pregnancy. It was a lonely time, and her mind went back to the time she had been raped in college. In her mind's eye she relived the beginnings of the rape. Then another image came, from a different direction. It was a light and within it a figure. She realized it was Jesus. Eagerly she hoped to see his face and find out what he really looked like. 'But as the figure came closer I found it impossible to see the face clearly. It wasn't just one face, but many faces appearing in rapid succession, too quickly for me to focus on any one countenance … I suddenly realized what this image was telling me: "See me everywhere, see me in everyone, look for me and you will find me." Upon receiving this thought I felt at peace, filled with joy. I continue to draw nourishment from that vision … and I continue to look for light beyond the fear.'

On the basis of this experience she concluded that

> Christ is the transformer, the reconciler, reconciling the opposites of victim and aggressor, male and female, reconciling all the divisions to which humanity is heir with the promise: 'Look for me and you will find me, everywhere in everyone.' The secret of Christ is that we live one life.

As I see it, we are born facing two ways at once: we are conscious of the universal ocean from which we sprang, but also confront ourselves as individuals. We are like the Roman god Janus, facing both ways at once. Reconciling that tension goes to my mind to the heart of human existence.

On the one hand, we alone (it appears) of the animal world are conscious of our own consciousness. Early in life we detach ourselves from the mother and develop a sense of our existential aloneness as a human being. The realm of consciousness we inhabit is unique and never fully sharable with or conveyable to others. At the same time, we are born with a sense of oceanic bliss, to which we seek to return, and which we always carry with us, if at times as little more than a distant echo. It is as though our task is to find our way back to unity, to the collective consciousness, through the spurious but inescapable sense of our individuality. This, surely, is what 'dying to the self' means – as never more powerfully symbolized than by the crucifixion.

At the heart of the mystical experiences on which the great faiths are founded is a revelatory knowledge that the world is not as it seems, combined with a sense of interrelatedness and oneness. In these moments we lose our sense of individuality and find ourselves instead swept up in a benign universe. This has been the experience of the mystics, as well as that of the innumerable 'ordinary' people whose lives have been changed by totally unexpected and inexplicable moments of mystical awareness in their lives.

The age of individualism

Ours, however, is the age of individualism. Of all the extraordinary changes that have taken place in the second half of this century, this has, perhaps, been the most profound of all. In no other era in history has there been such emphasis on the individual.

The trend towards individualism is something with which we are all familiar. Extended families living together are virtually a thing of the past. Elderly people are much less frequently looked after in the family, but either live alone or in homes for the elderly. Young people leave home at an earlier age, and more frequently spend some time as a single householder. A quite extraordinary range of individual behaviour, beliefs and modes of living is now tolerated as long as such conduct does not manifestly harm others. We talk of 'doing our own thing' in a way that would have been all but incomprehensible before the Second World War.

Parallel with the rise in individualism has been a decline in corporate religion. One of the hallmarks of our time is that 'doing our own thing' also extends to religion: as long as we feel, as individuals, that we are in touch with the spiritual side of life, that more or less ends the argument. The precise form it takes has become much less important than 'awareness' as such.

Ours is so much an age of individualism that it can be difficult to imagine or realize that people and societies ever approached life in any other way. And yet, the emphasis on the individual is comparatively recent, and largely bound up with the materialistic Western world.

The great flowering of the individual in Western culture is generally associated with the 18th century body of thought we know as the Enlightenment, but the seeds can in fact be traced back to the very roots of Western civilization and culture. Although there was an emphasis on community and 'relatedness' in the New Testament that is radically different from present-day perceptions (Newbigin 1984: 56), we are also dealing here unmistakably with the individual soul, in a way that was new and indeed revolutionary. In *advaita* Vedantism in the Hindu tradition, the notion of the individual, although wonderfully subtle, is very different: indeed, the illusory nature of the self and our apparent reality is a central theme in the writings of that greater unifier of Hindu thought, Vivekenanda (1862-1902) and the teachings of his master, Ramakrishna. The idea of the individual as we know it is also alien to Buddhism.

As we reach the end of the millennium, the fact that Western society is remorselessly driving us in the direction of the individual has, in my view, had a deeply disorienting effect. The beguiling siren-song of the individual has been at the expense of a sense of community and belonging, and has involved a certain loss of proportion. As Lorna Marsden puts it:

> The insistence of the self on its own unfettered autonomy is fostered by a kind of intoxication by which the self-recognizing brain distends its own meaning, thereby severing itself from the hidden roots of its being. This is the state of cerebral civilization of our century which has largely forgotten that the matrix of all existence lies in those reaches of Being where, beyond light and darkness, the Word of God is heard (Marsden 1995: 22).

In these circumstances, it is not surprising that God becomes even more of a Trickster. But unlike Job, we do not even rail against God, but dismiss the whole concept as illusion.

Ultimately, however, our extreme emphasis in this age on the individual may prove self-defeating, or be subject to a self-correcting mechanism. In our obsession with the individual, we find ourselves ineluctably drawn back to the greater whole – our other Janus face. Thus we find that an emphasis on self-awareness and individuation are central to contemporary society and the New Age movement. The latter is of particular interest because it combines an often extreme emphasis on the individual (with an ever growing variety of therapies, massages and treatments) with a consciousness of something wider, beyond our selves, as reflected in the concomitant emphasis on group work and group awareness. The New Age (in so far as one can speak of it collectively) has also drawn heavily on Eastern philosophy, western mysticism, alchemy and the occult, in all of which there is a marked emphasis on the unity of all things.

Opportunities
The New Age offers many opportunities for tapping into self-aware-

ness and, in the process, connecting up with the whole. Often, in modern therapeutic practice, there is a danger that a heightened sense of awareness of the whole has nowhere in particular to go and is left ungrounded as an essentially introverted experience – when it is in fact the very opposite. At their best, some of the new forms of self-discovery involve bringing ourselves as individuals to the group: which is of course precisely what Quakerism does. (It has always puzzled me that more New Age seekers do not make what would seem to be a logical progression – or sideways step! – to Quakerism.)

In many ways, our age is one of unparalleled opportunities. More perhaps than ever before, we now have the freedom to confront ourselves in the search for the Self. The path of inner awareness, self-realization and individuation that forms such an important aspect of the mystical tradition in all the great faiths has become a widespread aspect of our culture. There is, of course, the danger that the individual remains stuck in self-absorption, and the myriad New Age techniques and methods for exploring our selves are by no means always grounded in a spiritual framework, or may fail to provide any collective expression for the heightened self-awareness. Moreover, the emphasis in the wide variety of therapies that has sprung up over the past two or so decades is often not so much on losing or transcending the self as on functioning effectively as a personality. 'Wholeness' refers not to a sense of oneness but to feeling comfortable in ourselves and addressing the past experiences and psychological defence mechanisms we have built up and which hold us back as individuals.

But the integrity of the personality can, to my mind, never be fully achieved if we concentrate only on the individual and not on the whole from which we spring and to which we return – or more strictly we rediscover, as we never in fact leave it. The challenge of our age lies in confronting our existential aloneness while also tuning in to the infinite. Materialism and the focus on the individual have plunged our age into the upper reaches of spiritual endeavour, where the self is only 'lost', to discover the whole, through intense discipline, renunciation and the careful guidance of supportive communities. Ours may therefore be an age of unparalleled opportunities but it is also one of great potential for inner stress, confusion and ultimate unfulfilment – in short, for experiencing God as Trickster.

The Trickster and evolution

On the one hand, then, we have the atheism of the rational, scientific, Western world. (At its best this takes the form of humanism, bleak and blinkered though it is.) At the other extreme, we may regard the universe as a spiritual creation, in which we see through a glass darkly. There is, however, a possible third way between atheism and Trickster God, namely that spiritual awareness is itself part of the evolutionary process. This is the argument developed by an Australian microbiologist and biochemist, Darryl Reanney, in his book *The Death of Forever*. Reanney began with the scientific model, seeking to debunk the mystical, but in the end finds the two coming together. In the course of evolution,

> Man learned to externalise the inner workings of his mind, in symbols, on impressionable materials like clay, thereby fashioning a mirror to his own consciousness. From this came, I believe, a sense of ego-self, an ability to build a representational model of his own mental processes and so perceive himself in the act of perception (Reanney 1991: 90).

The urge for immortality becomes built into the ego-self. When we lose the false sense of self, death loses its meaning. As evolution has progressed, we have become more conscious of interconnectedness.

> Ego-self consciousness is, by its very nature, a passing phase. While consciousness is trapped in the ego-self prison, humanity remains perilously at risk from the destructive consequences of its own fragmented vision (Reanney 1991: 172).

In other words, the 'task' of evolution becomes a collective self-awareness, which we may call God. It is this dawning of awareness of our essential unity with all things at the expense of the separated-off self that is spirituality. Out of the void emerges the whole, mediated initially by the articulate entity of the 'individual', before moving to a more transcendent realm of collective consciousness.

That may be a distant vision, and in the meantime but very few of us manage to transcend the ego. Our scientific age necessarily places the observer – the illusory self – at the centre. Once that is done God of necessity becomes a Trickster. But every now and then, through no doing of our own, the whole breaks through the bounds of our individuality, and we are vouchsafed a glimpse of some greater realm. Those returning from such experiences often have a sense of complete certainty. They have been taken to a different realm of consciousness that is more real than the outward world they inhabit. Science may deride this, but science too finds itself increasingly driven towards a position ever closer to the mystical, as so brilliantly brought out by Fritjof Capra in *The Tao of Physics*. We must not reject what we cannot understand. That God is a Trickster is not due to any perversity on the part of God but is inherent in the human condition.

Going back to the analogy of the telescope, we are bound to mis-apprehend God as long as we do so from the vantage point of the individual. Here I believe that the great monotheistic religions are at variance with the testimony of their own mystical traditions when they proclaim the survival beyond death of the *individual* soul. As I see it, there are many tiers of consciousness, involving different degrees of separateness from the source. The soul returns to the all-embracing unity, and should not be seen in the strictly individualistic terms of our human existence. Here I feel more comfortable with the idea of the Group-soul, centred around a Spirit; each soul grows and evolves through the other souls associated with it as gatherers of experience.

The individual and the whole

We may think of the soul as a wisp of cloud attached to a greater cloud. On death, the wisp is drawn back into the greater cloud, with which it merges. The soul comes back to the mortal plane of existence in the sense of the cloud giving forth another wisp, which is not the identical wisp, but contains the experience garnered by the previous one, and also draws on the experience of the cloud, especially those parts close to it. This is why we can sometimes have a sense of recognition of an 'old soul' or 'soul-mate'.

If we see our spiritual side in these terms, the problem of God the Trickster disappears. With the merging of the apparently isolated, individual soul into the whole whence it came, God the Trickster becomes no more than a reflection of the illusion. It cannot be otherwise as long as we remain trapped in our sense of individuality – a sense we need for survival and everyday living. But once we see ourselves as drops in the ocean, or as coral islands poking up above the sea but conjoined on the seabed: once we do this, the injustice of the world and the unfairness of human existence, the conundrum of what happens to the soul of a baby who dies in infancy, and even the problem of good and evil, lose their meaning. The suffering of a peasant woman caught in ethnic cleansing becomes my suffering; my experiences, good and bad, joyful and disillusioning, are part of all humankind's experience, except that our perception of them is distorted by looking through the individual end of the telescope. Either God is a shabby fellow, or we must become shadowy fellows, when all falls away.

In a Seekers Association interest group on peak experiences, Grace Castle wrote of an occasion some 35 years before, at the age of 55. Falling into a deep meditation, she experienced a mystical sense of oneness with nature such as she had also felt at the age of four. Coming out of this expanded state of consciousness, she went in from the garden to fetch a drink. When she happened to glance in a mirror, 'I had a bewildering shock. The eyes that were reflected were my eyes, but it was not "I" that looked back. They were the eyes of Christ and I was shattered for they were full of compassion, but also grief. They looked through me to my weakness ... and the sins of mankind in general. Also they made me feel blessed so that I could go on and tread Life's path with confidence, with complete lack of fear, and dedication to the *Self*. The one-ness I feel with the natural world is now extended to the human family in general. Truly there is the One Life and we all share it.'

To me the great strength of Quaker meeting for worship is that it provides an opportunity for the individual to merge into a greater whole. We lose our selves in the gathered silence, which in turn forms part of a greater presence. Circles within circles, with the innermost circles dissolving as we lose our selves in the outer ones. It is that sense of unity found in the Quaker worship which, I firmly believe, explains why social action has always been an integral part of the Quaker experience. The Quaker concern is not with salvation or redemption but awareness. In the end, we can only accept the still inner voice and live in the mystery.

References

Arriens, J. *Welcome to Hell: Letters and Writings from Death Row*. Boston: Northeastern University Press, 1997.

Capra, F. *The Tao of Physics*. London: Fontana, 1976.

Johnson, R. *Watcher on the Hills*. London: Hodder and Stoughton, 1959.

Marsden, L. *The Singing of New Songs*. York: William Sessions, 1995.

Morris, C. *The Discovery of the Individual 1050-1200*. London: SPCK, 1972.

Newbigin, L. *The Other Side of 1984*. Geneva: WCC, 1984.

Reanney, D. *The Death of Forever: A New Future for Human Consciousness*. Melbourne: Longman Cheshire, 1991.

A Perfect Paradox

Kirsten Backstrom

Any human effort to conceive of God is paradoxical from the start. God is, by definition, larger than our human imagination. How can we possibly form a conception or create an image to adequately reflect the being that conceived and created us? How can we comprehend a God that is the very essence of ourselves, yet something far beyond ourselves? Our perceptions of God and our ideas about God are necessarily myriad and mercurial: we cannot limit God to a particular name; we cannot hold God to particular shape,

> there is no one unchanging idea contained in the word 'God'; instead, the word contains a whole spectrum of meanings, some of which are contradictory or even mutually exclusive. Had the notion of God not had this flexibility, it would not have survived to become one of the great human ideas (Armstrong 1994: xx).

If God is not merely a 'great human idea', but a great reality, then not only our 'notion of God' but the actual nature of God must also have this flexibility. Paradox is the ultimate expression of flexibility, and in paradox we see the Trickster nature of God at work.

What is the connection between the concept of paradox and the concept of God as Trickster? There are many definitions of the

Trickster, but virtually all of them must be essentially paradoxical. A Trickster is a contradictory being – one who reverses our expectations, using irreverent, playful, apparently careless conduct to bring about a fresh way of seeing and knowing, a shock of recognition, a larger comprehension. A Trickster takes us beyond ourselves by confronting us with ourselves in all our absurdity. The role of the Royal Fool (a quintessential Trickster figure) for instance, was to test the limits of the King or Queen's tolerance, to taunt and tease, to dance with danger like a kitten toying with a lion's tail, even to behave shamefully – and through this behavior, with a paradoxical grace and eloquence, to 'speak truth to power'.

I hope to demonstrate how God's presence as a Trickster-teacher can be experienced in the great and small paradoxes that make up our lives. If we can embrace or at least tolerate paradox, and learn to recognize it in the world, then we may catch a glimpse of something beyond the realm of ordinary perception and rational explanation. Paradox is not merely the coexistence of contradictions; it is what happens when irreconcilable truths come together so that their distinct qualities remain intact yet their differences are transcended. We can perceive God at work in the world, and at work within ourselves, through the leaping moment of comprehension that comes when an unprecedented, impossible new truth leaps out at us through a particular relationship of incongruities. Paradox has the multifaceted quality of a cut crystal which, when held to the light (or the Light), shows not only a distinct and separate reflection in each facet but also a brilliant projection of dancing rainbows.

In this essay, I will play the role of Royal Fool myself, using whatever comes to hand – from the crystal scepter to the chamber pot, from the exquisite to the ridiculous – bringing together disparate elements in contradictory ways to express the inexpressible. I will tumble around the throne room, first touching upon how we worship and approach God directly, then upon how God approaches us (directly and indirectly) through all kinds of paradoxical circumstances. As this essay develops, a particular focus will emerge: how the Trickster God is manifest in the great paradox of compassion. To illustrate throughout, I will use examples from Quaker history and Native American folklore; I will draw upon personal experience and also try to step back for a wider perspective.

I am making an effort to address some enormous, unanswerable questions: Why are our lives so comic and tragic? so contradictory? What is this paradoxical Trickster God all about? It is, of course, ultimately presumptuous and foolish to ask such things at all. Still, asking impossible questions, clumsily and cleverly, is one of our most perfectly human acrobatic techniques for coming close to the great mystery that is God.

✹

As Friends, one way that we address both the immanent God present in our lives and the transcendent God beyond us is in the context of our meetings for worship. We come together, each perhaps with a different understanding of what it is that we are doing here, yet all, if we are so blessed, sharing a present experience of God.

There is a certain absurdity in the very idea of worship: we 'wait upon' a God or Light that we can only imperfectly imagine. We share this experience with one another, and yet our experiences may be utterly different, even contradictory. A paradoxical leap of faith is required of us. We must hold ourselves in openness and readiness for an experience that is ultimately beyond our grasp.

The collective experience of worship is more than the sum of its parts. While we have all worshipped separately, a larger worship has occurred among us collectively as well – something beyond any single individual experience. This 'something beyond' is a perception of the presence of God: distinct in each of us, inexpressibly 'gathered' and expanded in all of us together.

A single dancer has a certain range of motion, but two dancers have far more than twice as many possibilities open to them, and with each additional dancer the possibilities for movement increase exponentially. In a similar way, when disparate or even divergent perceptions are brought together in worship, through the silence or through spoken ministry, the reaches of our spiritual imaginations may expand immeasurably.

George Fox's counsel on the subject of worship was often paradoxical. He generally wrote, and probably spoke, directly from his own rich and profound personal spiritual experience, and his words have the resonance of solid truth yet often seem to leave explicit, practical instruction aside; there is room for individual interpretation and application. This can be both confusing, when his meanings seem unclear, and compelling, when his language sweeps us along and invites us to follow our own leadings from God. In a letter of advice to convinced Friends, he wrote:

> In that which convinced you, wait; that you may have that removed you are convinced of. And all my dear Friends, dwell in the life, and love, and power, and wisdom of God, in unity with one another, and with God; and the peace and wisdom of God fill all your hearts that nothing may rule in you but the life which stands in the Lord God (Jones 1976: 232).

❂

In exploring the paradoxical nature of God the Trickster, I must begin with the body. Whether we approach God by listening for 'the still, small voice' within us, or by engaging more actively in prayer of thanksgiving, petition, intercession or praise – we must first dispose our bodies to attend. In a gathered meeting for worship, in a spirit of deep reverence, our stomachs may nevertheless be rumbling; we may find that we cannot help but cough; we may notice that our neighbor is fidgeting. Outside of meeting for worship, if we are trying to 'pray without ceasing' by treating each moment with a prayerful attention, how do we deal with those moments when we seem to be at the mercy of our bodies, our emotions, our circumstances?

If our hands are 'God's hands' (God's means of working in the world) then why would they ache and stiffen with arthritis? Why, when we have tried to take such good care of our physical, emotional and spiritual health are we afflicted with all kinds of ailments – from indigestion or allergies, to cancer or AIDS? Why does God present us with the paradox of our own imperfect bodies and lives? This seems to be a pointless sort of trickery. Is our God mocking us with such ridiculous gifts as hiccups, flatulence, acne, absent-mindedness? Even if we put the question of the meaning of human suffering aside for the moment, what can be the possible use of all the embarrassing, painful, inconvenient, uncomfortable or awkward aspects of being human?

I am not going to attempt to answer these questions directly, because they are unanswerable. It is pointless to try to 'resolve' a paradox. Instead, I want to present the incongruities in such a way that, I hope, God may be glimpsed at work, or at play, in the midst of them. Paradox accomplishes an impossible sleight of hand, a perfect trick: it presents opposite or contradictory truths all at once. Before our eyes, there is the reality of the body's manifest integrity as a conduit for God's life-energy, and there is the crude, clumsy, even ugly reality of the body's limitations. These contradictory realities are connected by the word 'and' – not by 'but', they do not detract from each other, they expand and emphasize each other. And so, through paradox, God offers us a glimpse of a truth beyond what common sense alone would allow.

✸

Several years ago, after being very sick for a long time, I was diagnosed with Hodgkin's Disease – a lymphatic cancer. For me, having a life-threatening illness was an extraordinary opportunity. As I went through chemotherapy and radiation treatments, I experienced every moment with overwhelming vividness and richness, and found a sense of larger and deeper meaning in even the most mundane or miserable moments. And, at the same time, my illness was filled with experiences of humiliation, pain, grief, despair, frustration, and fear.

The 'good' and the 'bad' qualities of my experience, the mundane and the profound, all came together. I could lie still for hours finding infinite delight in the way that light struck through the window and fell on the blanket; yet simultaneously I could be squirming with pain and nausea, longing for something to distract me from the intensity of the moment. I could feel sheer love, gratitude and tenderness as my partner stroked my back to soothe me to sleep; yet simultaneously I could feel a desperate grief and anxiety at the thought of what I was putting her through, the helplessness we both felt as my body wrestled with cancer.

My sense of the presence of God (an unpredictable Trickster of a God) was constant during this time. And this sense of presence did not come through the joyful side of things alone; it came through the paradox of the joy and the pain coinciding. I sensed something that went beyond the joy and the pain, something larger than either. Paradoxically, this seemed to be an experience greater than my own capacity for experience. It was certainly greater than anything I can describe. So, I will try to tell of it through stories, through my own sorts of Trickster tales, through instances of particular contradictions.

✦

One afternoon, at the peak of my chemotherapy treatments, I went out for a walk in an effort to distract myself from severe nausea. The anti-nausea medicine I'd been taking only worked provisionally and its effects wore off quickly; I was doing my best to get through the last hour before I could take another dose. Walking was difficult because I was extremely weak. Periodically, I would stop and sit down on the curb and weep almost absent-mindedly, because I seemed not to have strength enough to go any further. I knew that I presented a strange and disturbing spectacle to passersby: a gaunt, shivering, bald young woman sitting on the sidewalk weeping. I felt embarrassment and loneliness when I saw how people turned away from me, yet I also felt a detached understanding that I was doing my best and that they were doing their best as well, and that it was not necessary to explain the situation to myself or anyone else.

By the time I reached home, my knees were trembling with exhaustion and I was ferociously dizzy and nauseated. My left arm was in a sling because my first chemotherapy treatment had leaked from the vein and damaged nerves and tissue; my other arm had taken all of the chemotherapy since then, and it was badly bruised, with the hand cramped and weakened. I fumbled my keys out of my pocket with that hand and struggled to still my trembling so I could fit the door key into the lock. Then I tried to turn the key, but the lock was tight and my hand did not have the strength. Weeping with frustration and desperation, I fought with that stiff, unmoved key for what seemed ages. I stopped and sat down and sobbed, then stood and tried again. Finally, the bolt turned and I was in.

My anti-nausea medication was there on the table, but as soon as I picked up the bottle I knew that I was in trouble. The child-proof cap was twisted tight: with my hands in this condition, I could not open it. Again, I struggled, cried. I thought of breaking the plastic bottle with a hammer, but with my shaking hands I was afraid I would crush some of the pills or scatter them everywhere (the pills cost about $20 apiece and were precious).

Finally, I took the pill bottle and went out into the neighborhood, knocking on doors, looking for someone who might be home on a weekday afternoon to help me. About a block away, a young man answered his door and, looking at me with mingled suspicion and compassion, he opened my medicine. I went home, crying with relief now, and also laughing at myself and the situation.

During the hour or so that this adventure took, I was a walking paradox. I was utterly abject, helpless; and I was detached, curious about what would happen next, gently amused. I noticed nothing but my own misery; and I noticed that I was being humbled, challenged, shown the world and my neighborhood from an entirely new perspective. I was humiliated by appearing as a beggar on a stranger's doorstep; and I was touched by the simple humanity of our interaction. Peculiarly, I felt grateful not only for the relief of taking my medication and lying down safely at home, but also for the experience itself as a whole.

When my own hands failed me, I found myself 'in the hands of God'. Ultimately, I was handled with care, respect, protective reassurance … yet, God had also handled me rather roughly, as a puppy plays with a slipper.

❂

When I speak of God 'handling me roughly', I am speaking metaphorically, rather than literally. I don't think of God as a being who determines or even influences my personal experiences in this direct sort of way. Instead, I feel that I'm 'handled' by God in the same sense that I am 'handled' by life itself. There are patterns that emerge in life, and I believe that such patterns are meaningful. This meaningful tendency toward pattern and purpose is what I recognize as God interacting with our experiences. Perhaps how we interpret and respond to this interaction is what gives our relationship to God its fluid, unpredictable, tricksterish quality.

My own interpretation of my interaction with God is characterized by paradox. I am reminded of the apparently contradictory biblical phrase, 'I believe. Help thou my unbelief' (Mark 9: 24). Although I feel a sense of deep 'rightness' and ultimate faith in this God of pattern and purpose, enough belief to address God in my own mind as present being, the very nature of my belief is that it is reinforced (or diminished) by my own willingness (or unwillingness) to flow along with experiences and meanings I do not understand. The raw (sometimes very raw) material of experience offers opportunities for belief through unbelief: while absolute certainties can close our minds to revelations of truth that do not fit our preconceptions, acknowledging our doubts and confusion, our unbelief, can leave us room for new and surprising interactions with God. Only by trusting in the midst of my unbelief can I learn to interact with the tricky unreasonable aspects of my life, and thus find openings to God beyond the grasp of my reason.

❂

In much Native American Trickster lore, the Trickster is a figure not only of mystical power and great creative energy, but also and equally a ridiculous, malicious, petty, and downright vulgar sort of character.

> Trickster is at one and the same time creator and destroyer, giver and negator, he who dupes others and is always duped himself ... He knows neither good nor evil yet he is responsible for both. He possesses no values, moral or social, is at the mercy of his passions and appetites, yet through his actions all values come into being (Radin 1973: *xxiii*).

Coyote, for instance, is one Trickster that Quakers might find it hard to reconcile with God in any sense. As often as not, Coyote's greed, impatience, lust, or temper lead him to be the ultimate victim of his own tricks. And, at the same time, this trickery has a wonderful faculty for leading to larger meanings, larger acts of creativity and wonder. Through the most petty acts, the highest purposes are revealed, the highest ends are achieved.

Paradoxically, Coyote stories often use rude, irreverent humor to present subjects for which the tellers of these stories have the utmost reverence and respect. While Coyote is lying, stealing, defecating copiously, cheating, losing his penis, or getting himself killed in all sorts of hideous ways – the very universe is brought into being. Coyote's antics are responsible for the origins of certain sacred landmarks, human and animal characteristics, cosmic events. Coyote places the stars in the sky and gives names to all things, while at the same time making a complete fool of himself.

Any conception of the divine must take the existence of ugliness and absurdity somehow into account. However, the God of pure Light that many Friends embrace does not wear the mask of Coyote easily. Perhaps we are looking for a clean clarity, a 'perfection', in our relationship with God, and we may be disappointed if we try to apply that ideal to our everyday experience. Yet, the experience of disappointment and the failure of our ideals can be essential to the wholeness that true perfection entails.

The belief that perfection is attainable within our human lives is one of the original tenets of Quaker thought. But our definition of perfection must have a tricksterish flexibility and breadth. Even the most saintly lives are rather messy, filled with the body's demands, the heart's perplexities, the world's troubles. Any conception of the 'perfect' must take this messiness into account, must allow for lives in motion, in dissolution and perpetual regeneration. Paradoxically, perfection is a condition that always leaves room for us to be more perfect. The Trickster God has made us a potentially perfect world; the essence of that 'perfection' is in its potentiality – it is always in the process of coming about, and we may participate in it only by growing along with it.

> Perfection is not a static state of self-satisfaction. It not only permits growth, it requires growth ... Perfection means simply living up to the measure of light that is given ... and if we are faithful to that, we shall be given more (Brinton 1994: 48).

❂

One of the early companions of George Fox experienced a fall from the highest of good intentions to the most abject failure. James Nayler was known as a preacher of tremendous power and sensitivity. He used the phrase 'the Lamb's war' in reference to the terrible struggle within each individual to manifest ideals in behavior and so guide others by a Christ-like example of uncompromising, fierce gentleness and discernment. He was known for his capacity to listen to others with respect, and to inspire others by his own passionate earnestness. He refused to judge the leadings of others, even when those leadings mystified him, but trusted that ultimately God would distinguish the true leadings from the false and would even, potentially, put the false to good use. He rigorously humbled himself through long fasting, and exhausting efforts of prayer and preaching.

Yet, in spite of, or because of, his good intentions, he allowed himself to participate in an act that was seen as blasphemous hubris. His over-enthusiastic followers ushered him into Bristol in a scene that mimicked Jesus's arrival in Jerusalem: Nayler riding horseback while his followers cast their clothes in the mud before him and sang of his holiness. This exhibition was probably not his own idea, yet he did not put a stop to it. Paradoxically, his humility in honoring the leadings of others prevented him from dismounting and walking away from them; perhaps he even allowed himself to be worshipped (an act of the utmost hubris) out of the deepest sense of humility. As a result of this action, he was judged before Parliament and received a horribly harsh sentence.

> He was to be set in the pillory in Palace Yard, Westminster … for two hours, and then whipped by the hangman through the streets of the Old Exchange. Two days later he was to stand in the pillory at the Old Exchange for two hours and have his tongue bored through with a red-hot iron and have his forehead branded with a B. Afterwards he was to be sent to Bristol, carried through the city on a horse bare-ridged, with his face backwards, and publicly whipped in the market place. Finally he was to be imprisoned indefinitely in solitary confinement with hard labour, without pen, ink or paper, until released by Parliament. James Nayler heard this sentence with dignity. 'God has given

me a body,' he said. 'He will, I hope, give me a spirit to endure it ...' (Vipont 1954: 58).

In addition to these punishments, Nayler was personally shamed by an awareness that his actions had damaged the efforts of other Friends to establish the legitimacy of their faith in a country where religious persecution was rampant. After years in prison, he made a great effort to expose his own shame and humble himself still further, in order to win back the trust of his friends.

Yet the words that he wrote or spoke as his 'last words' (probably not an actual deathbed speech, but meant to represent the culmination of his life and belief) were about the gift of ultimate humility, the experience of God to be found in deep suffering.

It is also paradoxical to consider in retrospect that Nayler's ride into Bristol turned out to be an essential crossroads in early Quaker history. Because of his extreme example, Friends were forced to clarify their understanding of discernment, and to emphasize the distinction between personal impulses and true leadings (a distinction that was often blurred among other sects like the Ranters). Politically, Quakers became stronger and clearer after Nayler's fall, although at the time his actions endangered their very survival. And Nayler himself both suffered terribly and received a kind of grace.

❂

It may appear (and may be true) that God played a cruel trick on James Nayler. What had the man done to deserve such a brutal 'fall from grace?' With disturbing regularity, those whose efforts are greatest on behalf of God are the ones subjected to the harshest treatment by God. From Job to Jesus, from the martyrs of history and myth to many more ordinary folks in modern times – the 'good' are the ones to suffer. But there is another way to look at this paradox.

According to Buddhism, suffering is at the very heart of human experience – not only for the saintly, but for all. And the solution to the problem of suffering has little to do with eliminating the conditions of suffering (which are universal) but with eliminating the 'desires' (attachments to transitory things) that cause us to experience these conditions as suffering.

So, perhaps certain exceptional people are subjected to the most graphic extremes of suffering precisely because they are able to detach themselves and transform this suffering into something higher, to extract a deeper meaning from it, a larger experience of faith and love than would ordinarily be possible. Those who suffer greatly can be perfect examples for the rest of us with our more commonplace suffering, that such faith and love are possible, not only in spite of the harshness of life, but in a sense through the harshness of life.

Obviously, this kind of idea can be badly misapplied and abused. There have been plenty of fanatics over the years who have inflicted appalling tortures on themselves in an effort to 'mortify the flesh', expiate sins, or reach God. And it would generally not be useful to a person suffering from a terrible disease or disaster nowadays to be told that they should experience this suffering as a gift. Yet suffering can be literally both a gift and an affliction. As with any paradox, this sounds patently absurd in the abstract; it can only be experienced directly, grasped experientially.

While it is simplest to see grace as the easing of suffering, and God as the reliever of suffering, a direct experience of God actually transcends suffering without necessarily eliminating it, and this can only really be understood or believed if one has experienced pain and deep spiritual joy simultaneously.

✵

At various times during my own experience with cancer, I had tiny glimpses of the kind of transcendence that may be found through suffering. There were many miserable and painful side effects from chemotherapy, radiation, and the cancer itself that left me exhausted and often despairing – but almost always when these troubles reached a pitch that seemed unendurable, there would be a kind of breakthrough: not an easing of symptoms, but a shift in attitude and a sense of peace.

During the six weeks when I was receiving high daily doses of radiation, I experienced my whole body, in fact my whole being, in a state of continuous suffering. My oesophagus was being badly burned by the treatments, so I could not swallow solid food, and swallowing even small amounts of liquid was very painful. There was a constant trickle of saliva running down the back of my throat, and I was perpetually fighting the gag reflex and the impulse to swallow repeatedly. If I became preoccupied by this sensation, I would begin to choke: gagging, coughing, and hiccupping convulsively. The skin on my chest, back, and neck was burned. I was weak and nauseated, hungry but unable to eat, and deeply depressed as a result of the helplessness I felt.

One day, all of this reached an unbearable pitch, and I found myself hunched miserably on a kitchen chair trying to choke down a dose of liquid pain medicine, fighting tears because crying itself was painful. I felt utterly sorry for myself, and it seemed that there was absolutely no point in being alive when things were this bad.

But, in the moment of having this thought, it occurred to me simply and immediately that my very helplessness was a unique and incredible opportunity. There was absolutely nothing I could do in that moment but let go and experience being alive – I was not responsible for imparting meaning to my life, for 'doing' anything in the world, for proving anything to myself or anyone else. I was not, at that moment, capable of doing or being any of the things I'd always identified with; no label would fit, not even my name. And, paradoxically, this absence of identity and attachment filled me with a deeper sense of individuality. I felt myself as a 'soul', flowing from God and returning to God. No aspect of my true self was lost, only an old, superficial skin was sloughed off. There was also that indescribable sense of a presence that went beyond myself – a perception of God as something or someone real and immediate, not human-like at all, but of an entirely 'other' order of being. I experienced this not in a flash of illumination, but in a deep yet familiar and almost ordinary certainty and trust.

The entire process of my illness was an encounter with the prospect of my own eventual death, and the physical and emotional suffering I experienced along the way was in a sense an experience of death on a small scale: the erasure of immediate ego-identity and the glimpse of another sort of identity beyond.

> In the aloneness, the isolation, the singling out, the individuating process of death, there is an emergence of what it means to be the responsible bearer of a life design (Steere 1943: 130).

Nevertheless, I want to emphasize that my physical suffering was not eased in the slightest by this realization of a larger order of being. In fact, I was very much aware of my body's misery, and very much afraid of identity-loss and ultimately of death, but I also felt a deep compassion for that misery, as though it were happening to someone else. I was able to perceive that true compassion was expansive enough to include all suffering, not merely my own.

✪

How can the divine compassion of God encompass the horrors of human suffering? Of course, this is a paradox that theologians and religious seekers of all kinds have wrestled with for centuries. Whether God is seen as a Father-creator or a Light or a Trickster or something still more indescribable, God is generally perceived as an embodiment of compassion. In a recent workshop on Quaker faith as it relates to death and dying, we were asked to speak of our most basic assumptions and beliefs. One particular phrase was repeated by many of those present: 'God is love'.

Yet the universe seems so unloving! Not only are there horrors like genocide and torture, but the simple reality of all of our lives is that we will die, and that death involves loss: both emotional and physical pain. We will all, in the course of our lifetimes, suffer pain in varying degrees, and for most of us there will be at least brief experiences of excruciating pain. We will all lose people we love, and suffer large and small tragedies of many kinds.

I have always found the Buddhist concept of universal suffering a bit hard to swallow, since I am fairly optimistic and tend to enjoy life most of the time – but it is also clear that the worst misery that any person on earth has suffered is not alien to my own experience. Pain and grief are inevitable, and every time we love or feel joy we are opening ourselves to the pain of an ending. My reverence for the beautiful things in my life is tempered, and strengthened, by the awareness that I cannot keep them. Although I have survived one bout with cancer, I know that this very body that I think of as 'myself' will sometime within the next thirty years or so, sooner or later, die and disintegrate. I know that the work I've done and the love I've felt in the world will be absorbed into something larger, as a wave settles back into the sea. I can only trust and hope that some personal essence extends beyond this lifetime. But I do not know what such an essence might consist of – and I feel sure that it will not include most of the features of my present identity.

However, the idea that pain, sorrow and transience make this an 'unloving' sort of world is only a superficial judgment. In fact, the greatest paradox of all seems to lie in the fact that pain and sorrow are just as much at the heart of God as are joy and contentment. Compassion unites grief and love in a perfect paradox. It is a state of sheer intimacy and openness in the face of deep suffering: it is a transcendence of separateness that comes about through the most palpable experience of separateness.

❁

After the nerve injury to my arm during chemotherapy, I had several weeks of intense pain, which could fortunately be controlled by keeping the whole arm literally half-frozen, with the constant application of ice packs. Since the pain could be turned on and off with ice, and since it was confined to a limited area, it offered me an opportunity to experiment with my own pain thresholds and with pain management techniques. At one point, I worked with a friend who is a therapist, in an effort to further explore what pain actually is and how to cope with it.

We began by setting the ice pack aside, and he asked me to focus on the sensations that developed in my arm. In a short time, the pain was enough to make my breathing rapid and shaky, and I had a frantic impulse to retrieve the ice pack and stop the whole experiment. I resisted and held on, as my heart started to race and I broke out in a sweat. It felt as if the tissues of my arm were shot through with electricity. It felt as if the veins in my arm were pulsing and swollen with a molten liquid. A moment later, these specific sensations gave way to a vast, dizzying spiral of pain, like a hot, harsh light that swirled all around me, sucking me down.

Still, my friend urged me to enter the pain itself, to imagine walking right into it. He suggested that once I was inside of it, the pain would change and end. It did not happen like that. Instead, as I imagined walking into the pain, the light brightened and the pain increased.

And then, I was aware that I seemed to be experiencing this from two distinct perspectives at once. I was in the very center of the pulsing pain – burning alive, absorbed utterly by suffering. And, I was also aware of this suffering as if from the outside, observing it. As soon as I recognized this larger point of view, I felt a rush of empathy and protectiveness towards the part of me that was suffering.

The suffering was increasing steadily as I watched, yet at the same time I could observe this suffering objectively, with complete detachment. It's too bad that 'objectivity' and 'detachment' are the only words available to describe this feeling; in our everyday language these words imply a kind of coldness, an absence of caring. In fact, however, the particular kind of objectivity I am trying to describe was anything but cold, anything but neutral. It was a paradox of compassion – a huge tenderness toward the one suffering pain, yet a detachment that made this tenderness expand to include all pain suffered by anyone, ever.

I am trying to describe the indescribable. The pain was very real, and it grew all-encompassing – not only my own pain, but the essence of pain itself. And yet the compassion was just as vast. I felt that I comprehended, with grief and tenderness, the meaning of all this pain, and could see no separation between myself and every other being who has ever suffered. The suffering and the love both seemed to be essential to what we are at the deepest level. And God seemed to be present in the brilliance of this profound, paradoxical compassion.

This was rather overwhelming, of course, and yet it was only a brief, easy step away from ordinary experience. My friend and I sat in his living room; someone upstairs was moving furniture; it was raining outside. But the power of the experience was real and we both felt it. I couldn't have adequately described the sensations to my friend and didn't try, yet we both felt the compassion and both entered into it or were gathered in by it. For perhaps half an hour, we sat there sharing the pain and beaming with joy. And then it seemed time to return to normal. My arm hurt and I had had enough. I put the ice pack back on and went home to sleep for a long time.

✹

I've been self-conscious about recounting this experience of compassion before now, because I'm afraid that if I cannot express the paradoxical nature of it, then it will simply seem melodramatic if not megalomanic. Here are the pieces of the paradox, all tumbled together like chips of colored glass in the lens of a kaleidoscope: the experience was extraordinary, and it was an experience available to anyone, anytime; it was a help to me personally in coping with pain, and it was not about my private pain at all but something in comparison with which my own pain was nothing.

If peering into the kaleidoscope of this experience gave me a glimpse through pain to something larger, it was certainly not a revelation uniquely bestowed on me; it was more of a demonstration of how God is present as an essential part of our very humanness, something that is both within and beyond all of us without distinction. Compassion is entirely different from pity: it allows for no separation between the sufferer and the compassionate one, between the needy and the needed. I can only begin to understand it after having had a small experience of what it is like. It is the capacity in each individual to truly know the nature of pain in others and in ourselves – to grasp our shared humanness, and begin to comprehend the truth expressed by the words 'God is love'.

✪

The shortest Bible verse contains this paradox of compassion in two words. Upon hearing that his friend Lazarus was dying or already dead, and before going out to heal him and bring him back to life, 'Jesus wept' (John 11: 35). For me, these words make Jesus a real person, and also a symbol of something utterly wonderful: an expression of human pain and divine compassion at once. Jesus could have known that he was capable of healing Lazarus; he could have seen beyond the immediate loss, to a larger life. And yet, even as he was on his way to give life, he was overwhelmed with grief and love for the suffering and death of his friend.

From the perspective of something as wide and deep as God, any individual suffering is only a brief, tiny, inconsequential thing – over and forgotten in a moment. And, at the same time, any and every instance of suffering is of incomparable significance. We, as human beings, can and must experience sufferings, losses, and deaths as vividly real and terrible; and we are also given a share, through compassion, in God's capacity to both apprehend and transcend even the greatest grief.

✪

This essay into paradox has been taking the form of a Trickster's tumbling: from a 'gathered meeting' to a passage through extreme illness; from Coyote to James Nayler; from personal experience to cosmic speculation. Now, after approaching such deep and serious subjects as human suffering and divine compassion, I feel the need to conclude on a lighter note.

Consider again the character of the court jester, the Royal Fool: a figure of paradox and trickery. In former times, the role of Fool was a special and prestigious one, requiring great mental and physical dexterity. The Fool's job was to amuse the Queen or King, and also, in a subtle and ingenious manner, to act as a check upon abuses of royal power and privilege. The clever Fool could advise and even reprimand the King through riddles, limericks and mimicry. The Fool could strut about mocking the King's behavior, because the Fool was the most abjectly humble of all the King's minions.

In a sense, the Fool was only an extension of the royal personality, made manifest. The Queen could see her own smallness, silliness, and ultimate Foolishness, in the figure of her Fool – and so she would excuse the Fool as she would excuse herself, and correct the Fool as she would correct herself, and laugh at the Fool as she would love to be able to laugh at herself, and learn from the Fool as she would learn from the cleverest parts of herself if she were not inhibited by the weightiness of her royal role.

For a final paradox, a last trick, let's try to look at this Foolishness from two sides at once. First, let's suppose that we human beings are God's Fools: we bumble about in a ridiculous parody of the greatness of God, while God watches us, laughs at us, loves us, forgives us and learns from us.

Now, let's reverse ourselves and suppose that God is humanity's Fool instead. God is the Trickster. We, the Kings and Queens, are regally puffed up with the grandeur of our own roles and responsibilities, and God is the one who sees through us, plays along with us, and ultimately shows us what we really are.

Out from a dark corner of our dank throne room, this ragged, colorful, deft, clever God comes tumbling. This God knows that we are preoccupied with weighty affairs, that we are genuinely struggling with our decisions, and that we are perhaps suffering with deep griefs of our own, yet this God comes before us all in a rush, trips over the royal red carpet and falls flat, then leaps up taunting and dancing and irreverently rhyming. This God somersaults through all of our temperamental responses – our annoyance, our amusement, our distraction – and winds up finally with our whole attention. Our God, our Fool, completes a series of flips and cartwheels, then stands before us with outspread arms – an acrobat concluding a perfect performance – to accept all of our responses, to know us absolutely, and to embrace us.

References

Armstrong, K. *A History of God: The 400-Year Quest of Judaism, Christianity and Islam*. New York: Alfred A. Knopf, 1994.

Brinton, H. *Friends for 300 Years*. Wallingford, Pennsylvania: Pendle Hill, 1994.

Jones, R., ed. *The Journal of George Fox*. Richmond, Indiana: Friends United Press, 1976.

Radin, P. *The Trickster: A Study in American Indian Mythology*. New York: Schocken Books, 1973.

Steere, D. *On Beginning From Within*. New York & London: Harper & Brothers, 1943.

Vipont, E. *The Story of Quakerism*. London and Richmond, Indiana: Bannisdale Press and Friends United Press, 1954.

A Trail of Tricks

Gay Pilgrim

Lord, forgive my little jokes on thee,
And I'll forgive Thy great big one on me
(Frost 1979: 428)

Introduction

In this chapter I outline very briefly my understanding of the nature of God and God's use of tricks. I go on to relate particular instances from my personal experience which have felt like tricks, culminating in one which resulted in an experience of such impact that it has totally changed my life. I attempt to explain what this change has meant for me, and then reflect, in the light of this, how I interpret and understand what such tricks are about. I conclude with where I am now in my understanding of, and relationship with, God.

When I was asked to consider contributing a chapter to a book on God as Trickster, I thought there was only one occasion I could put my finger on when I could clearly see God as tricking me. In the process of thinking about how to write of this experience, I began to realise that this, as much as any other interaction with Life and God, depends on the perspective adopted. This realisation was spurred along by reading Margaret Guenther's *Holy Listening* in which she writes:

> when I first sought ordination I was sure that my
> ministry lay with the dying, most probably in the
> institutional ministry of hospital, nursing home or
> hospice. To find myself again in academe seemed ... a
> sign of divine humour (Guenther 1996: 4).

It made me take another look at my life and re-view the ordinary
events which, whilst they have seemed so wonderfully ironic, I have
never associated with God.

To see God as a Trickster or Hoaxer seems to me to presume that
God intervenes actively in our lives, that God sets out to provoke
and challenge us into 'awareness' by presenting us with situations
which are hardly what we would wish. When tricked by a human one
can either laugh or cry, feel angry or impressed. The same is true of
my response to God, yet I have great difficulty with the idea that
God is so minutely active in the details of our individual lives. So I
live with conflict as my intellect opposes my experience; and discomfort as my reason attempts to make sense of the tension of
believing simultaneously in an actively interventionist God, and in an
accessible but non-interventionist God.

Of course there is always the danger of attributing too much to
God. Much of what happens to us we bring upon ourselves, and it
has been a helpful discipline to winnow out all those times when I
could clearly see my own, albeit unwitting, contribution to events. I
was waiting to see emerge from the sifting those times which were
not in my control, and to review them in the light of the possibility
of Divine trickery. I am aware that with hindsight one can perceive
all sorts of meanings and obtain all manner of insights to which one
was wholly oblivious at the time; but if one had not been ignorant,
could one have been tricked?

A brief look through the Hebrew scriptures throws up many
occasions when God plays tricks on people, and the greatest of these
must be the life of Job – a whole book devoted to the lessons to be
learned through trickery. How can one *not* see God in this way?

The lengths God seems to be prepared to go to in order to reach us seem quite extraordinary to me. Look at Abraham and Isaac: God's trick on Abraham with regard to Isaac (or was the trick on Isaac?) was a very risky strategy. Abraham learned the lesson of faithful obedience when God's commands not only made no sense (after all wasn't Isaac given to Abraham and Sarah by God?), but were totally antithetical to everything Abraham held dear.

When considering whether God is a Trickster or Hoaxer I return again and again to Genesis, where we are told that humans are made in God's image; so it is not entirely unreasonable to suppose that just as we have a sense of humour, and enjoy teasing and trickery, so does God. Even if the concept of God as Trickster and Hoaxer is inconceivable for some, I think it is indisputable that paradox is real, and paradox can often feel like being tricked or hoaxed. The Scriptures are full of paradox, just as life is full of paradox. Love lives with hate. Difference can be simultaneously a blessing and a curse. Wisdom is also foolishness. To gain life, one must first lose it. Trickery can reveal truthfulness – does it also therefore fall into the category of paradox?

The nature of my God

I am aware that the 'nature' of God is a strongly contested area, and the characteristics I attribute to God may well not be so attributed by others. So what do I mean when I refer to a transcendent God? For me the transcendent God is best described in Psalm 138, verse 6 'too wonderful for me ... too high, beyond my reach' (*The Grail Psalms* 1990: 238). So I understand this version of God as being in everything and everywhere, but disinterested in my personal concerns, non-interventionist and not acting in my life in any specific concrete way, although always available to me and aware of me in a dimension I cannot begin to grasp. I realise that this understanding of God is not borne out in the whole of Psalm 138.

Quite the contrary in fact, but then one of the things I really love about the Hebrew scriptures is the extraordinary intimacy they express towards God. I haven't the courage or bravery to take this intimacy on board in the same way, and find it necessary to 'split' my God between a cosmic transcendent abstract Being, and an intimate, immanent, interventionist, guiding, and present Being. This immanent God is also well described further on in this psalm, 'O Lord, you search me and you know me, you know my resting and my rising ... Before ever a word is on my tongue you know it O Lord, through and through.' This God however is no less mysterious despite the greater sense of intimacy I experience, and once again this psalm says it for me: 'To me, how mysterious your thoughts, the sum of them not to be numbered! If I count them, they are more than the sand; to finish, I must be eternal like you.' The sense I have of being called, invited, and sometimes pushed, belongs to this immanent God. A God who seems not to hesitate to interfere, intervene, trick or hoax me, in order to ensure that I 'wake up!'

Tricks or tests

But 'wake up' to what? Why does God seem to hit me over the head with a sledgehammer to get my attention, and then seemingly abandon me with my head spinning and aching, to work out 'what on earth that was all about'? It is very often at this point that I forget that facing up to God requires courage and bravery, and I tend to shout very angrily and loudly to the effect, 'What did you do *that* for? And having done it how *dare* you just bunk off without telling me!' And God's response? Laughter! I hear laughter echoing through my soul. Don't tell *me* God's not a trickster.

In the process of pondering, musing, and reflecting on what these experiences can possibly mean, I have sometimes felt that it is not quite accurate to regard them as tricks. I might feel that I have been tricked, but equally might it have been a test? Perhaps the story of Abraham and Isaac is not a good example of a trick. It might more accurately be regarded as a test; and the Scriptures make it clear that Job was selected for God's contest with Satan because he was good material for such a *test*. Once again, it is the perspective through which we choose to view the events that informs our understanding of whether we have been tricked or tested. One might ask, 'what kind of a God would test us?' but that is to see a test as an examination, something one must either pass or fail. The *Collins Concise Dictionary* of 1998 offers us other possibilities, for instance 'to make an exploratory initial approach; find out'. My experience is that this latter description is a more accurate explanation of what is taking place for me. God makes the initial exploratory approach, and I do the finding out! It isn't a matter of passing or failing. We cannot 'fail' God. We cannot in reality even fail ourselves, though my personal experience is that I can, and do, fail others. My understandings of God, transcendent and immanent, are as Henri Nouwen describes in the parable of the prodigal son (Nouwen 1994). God's whole Being longs for us to turn towards the Light, to help us in our desire to live in the heart of God, to enable us to open our hearts and souls so that God's love can flow freely to us, through us, and out to others and all creation.

The failure, if failure there is, is in our lack of faith and trust that God really does love us unconditionally. It is certainly something that I fail in. For whatever reasons, most of my experience of human loving is that it is very, very far from being unconditional. It is therefore hard to even imagine what such a love might be, never mind to experience it through an unseen, often absent, and definitely nebulous God.

The trail

It has been necessary to be selective about my experience of God's tricks. To relate the whole trail would be to write my spiritual autobiography. Instead I offer a few snapshots; 'stills' of moments in time when I have felt God acting in my life in this way.

The first major trick was my father's death when I was ten years old. My father was a Roman Catholic who carried his belief in, and love of, God with a lightness of touch and a joyousness of spirit that shone through everything he did. He had a real love for humanity in all its guises, messy or glorious. He looked always for what Quakers term 'that of God' in everyone and lived out his beliefs in a practical and useful way.

He was also what today we call a 'universalist', believing that God valued and loved the diversity and difference between all the peoples of the world, and therefore was revealed in ways that could be understood within each cultural context. He showed me what it was to live lovingly. Of course he wasn't perfect, but to my ten year old eyes and heart he was, made all the more so because of the difficult and rather fraught relationship that I had with my mother – a relationship that brought out the worst in both of us. It could be said that my parents modelled two aspects of God: my father the loving, tender and compassionate aspects of God, my mother the demanding, contrary, jealous, critical, exacting, and punitive ones. She was also an atheist who found the whole notion of God ridiculous.

My father's death left me not only emotionally bereft, but spiritually rudderless. I was adrift in a world where the comfort I was offered was that 'only the good die young'. What was I to make of this? Was I being told that by being 'good' I would die? Was I being told that to be 'good' meant I would be annihilated? Or punished? What was it saying to me about the nature of God? What kind of a God would so prematurely 'take' someone who had so much love and joy in them? A greedy God? A selfish God? It was at this point in my life that I first became aware of major inconsistencies in the way God was presented to me. There was an all-loving, all-giving God who left us free will; a stern watchful God who apparently offered us a choice, but then punished us if we made the wrong one; and now an unpredictable and possibly capricious God. Up until my father's death I had had a simple and unquestioning faith. Suddenly I was faced with a God whose intervention seemed not only incomprehensible, but cruel. The God I had learned about through my father was a God of love, joy, compassion and justice. How could such a God wilfully and deliberately cause his death?

The need to make sense of, and find reasons for, what happens to us is very strong. The arbitrary nature of life is frightening. It would have been all too easy to have developed a theology of an all-seeing, all-knowing God who has a personal life-plan for each of us, a plan not given to us to understand, but to live as God dictates. It was certainly the most obvious theological interpretation to the kind of remark made to me that I should feel thankful God so loved my father that He had chosen to call him to his side so young. That I didn't adopt this theology may in part be due to the fact that it didn't correspond with my own 'knowing' of God; and in part to my mother's atheism. She was robust in her rebuttal of such comments, and of course she didn't blame God. How can you blame something that doesn't exist?

It seems to me that my father's death was a trick in the sense that it was a test directed at me – bearing in mind my definition of a test, that is 'to make an exploratory approach'. If God is searching for me always, then it will be in the chaotic events of everyday life that I shall be approached; but there are some moments which are more propitious than others, moments when we are more vulnerable, more open, more accessible to God, and more likely to notice and become aware. Being confronted by the reality of death no matter what one's age, is one of those moments. In the midst of my bewilderment, confusion and the numbing pain of loss, something happened. One day, when I was washing up at home, I had an overwhelming sense of a presence. I felt it so strongly that I turned around to say 'hello'. Ostensibly there was nothing there, but I knew there had been, and I understood that in some mysterious way I was being comforted and released to grieve. Looking back, it is clear to me that this was the first time God explicitly approached me and that this approach offered me the opportunity to realise that I had a choice about how to live out the effects of my father's death in my own life. I could choose to continue to love and trust, or I could choose to stay separate through mistrust. There was no-one to whom I could confide this experience and it became buried, tucked away with all the other memories associated with my father; so I made the latter choice, remaining separate and mistrustful.

The second trick was my marriage when I was 22. By this time I had given up on God, though not because of anything in particular, more a case of creeping indifference and increasing irrelevance. I hadn't stopped believing altogether, but I had become a definite 'don't knower' and termed myself agnostic. In retrospect I can see that God was continually present through others and circumstances, but I was neither listening nor looking. God had a lot of competition, since my formative adult years took place during the 'swinging sixties'. Like many of my contemporaries I embraced with enthusiasm the concepts of free love, peace and flower power. In some respects the ideals these represented are not so far from the Gospels. Loving others unpossessively, holding material goods in common, resolving conflicts peacefully instead of through aggression ... I might argue that the motivation, the energy behind these ideals was falsely based, but nevertheless there was a passionate longing for a better world, a fairer world, a more just world; a longing common to Quakers and *all* those who seek to bring about 'God's reign on earth'. Could this period of history have been one of God's tricks/tests on humanity as a whole? Did we collectively miss the opportunity and the mark? Interestingly Doug Gwyn has suggested to me in conversation that there *are* moments in time when God can break through to us collectively, but so far we have missed that moment.

I hadn't anticipated getting married. Indeed I didn't wish to get married. As an active member of the Women's Movement it was very clear to me that being married was likely to damage my health. Moreover, how could I make promises that were meaningless to me? The concept of monogamy implied ownership, possession, and an exclusiveness that had little personal appeal, and the idea of permanence even less so. So why did I get married? It was pointed out to me that if I really believed marriage was so immaterial and unimportant, then it shouldn't make any difference to me whether I was married or not. There seemed a logic to that, and having been told by my Australian Army fiancé that it was impossible for an Australian soldier to just live with a woman, I agreed to go through a civil ceremony on the clear understanding that I wouldn't regard myself as bound in any way, shape or form, even though I had signed a contract. We were duly married – prophetically, in a little town called Battle.

The history of the relationship is relevant only insofar as our attempts to resolve its difficulties led to us accepting a job with the World Health Organisation in Papua New Guinea, in a mission field. We were working and living amongst missionaries of every description: Catholics, Seventh Day Adventists, Anglicans, Methodists, Baptists, and other non-conformists whose denominations now escape me. There were those whose lives did indeed 'speak' to me, and by whom I was sufficiently impressed to be willing to attend their services of worship. I enjoyed the many discussions and stimulating conversations over meals about God and faith. The depth of joy, lovingness and compassion demonstrated by those who became our friends made an indelible impression on me, and they unquestionably mediated God's love to me. Not once did they attempt to convince or convert us. Not once did they make us feel 'outsiders', 'unsaved', or 'damned', despite their own beliefs. In terms of being 'tested', God was clearly approaching me from every angle and I was definitely in a place where I had the greatest possible opportunity to both see and feel God's call. It was also one of those moments in time when I was extremely vulnerable because I was so deeply miserable in my marriage, desperately searching for some kind of way to remain in it until our two young children had grown up. Hence my supposition that my marriage was one of God's 'tricks'. If I hadn't married that particular man I wouldn't have been living in a place where God was so variously represented; where people truly gave up their lives to God; where God's love was made visible through their lives. What greater opportunity could I have been given to turn towards God? But if it was a trick then it failed, because I turned away from God's approach. I left my marriage and returned to England. I wasn't yet ready to respond to God's invitation. I wasn't yet ready to choose to love and trust.

The third trick caused my move to Shropshire: a move which I believe resulted in my becoming a Quaker. I had been given a significant sum of money to use as a deposit for a mortgage so that I could buy my own home and move out of my Housing Association flat in London. Even so, it was insufficient for me to be the sole mortgage holder, so in order to stay in London I decided to co-buy with a friend. We had what seemed a very sensible contract binding us to the house for five years; this being the time it would take my daughter to complete her secondary education at a nearby school. There was a 'let out' clause, but neither of us expected to need it. I was shocked when it was invoked by my co-buyer a little over a year after we took up residence. He had met his now wife, who was less than happy with our arrangement, inevitably perhaps. The irony turned out to be that I could have bought on my own after all. I only discovered *after* the co-purchase of the house had been completed that, as a Housing Association tenant, I had been eligible for a 30 per cent reduction in a mortgage which would have enabled me to purchase a property independently.

One might ask how this could be conceived of as a trick by God, rather than the result of my own ignorance or failure to obtain all the information available. My response is that God appears to have moved me to the oddest places before attempting to break through to me. I believe that if I had not left London for Shropshire, I would not have had the time or the space to perceive the wonderful and beautiful world we live in: a world which both reflects and connects me with God, a world which opens me up to the mystery and wonder of life, a world which speaks to my heart and soul and not my head, a world which made it possible for me to respond to God's approach.

At the time of my relocation I considered myself an atheist, and certainly wasn't seeking or looking for God. I discovered only after I had moved that Shropshire is a 'black hole' in terms of work, but unemployment gifted me the opportunity to go for long walks in the countryside and to be alone. It was a time of replenishment, physically and spiritually, as I rediscovered a sense of the phoenix-like nature of creation. The eternal cycle of life and death – the amazing, astonishing, miraculous renewal of life after apparent death, visible in the burgeoning forth of spring. For me the story of the Resurrection holds little meaning, but as I watch this miracle each year, something nags at me and I know that there is a mystery here that God will at some point require me to engage with. Something (God?) nagged at me then, and to my surprise I found myself one Sunday morning sitting in the Quaker Meeting. I felt then, and feel now, that I was 'grabbed' by God. It was as if God finally lost patience, picked me up by the scruff of the neck, dumped me down in Shrewsbury Meeting and said 'Sit!' I have since wondered why Quakers, rather than another church, and can only assume that God understood that, had I been exposed to explicit 'God language' at that point, I would have run again. As it was, I was given *Questions and Counsel* to read, not *Advices and Queries*. At that time British Friends were in the process of revising this little booklet (designed to be read regularly as an aid to living faithfully) and had more or less eliminated any 'God language' in the *Questions and Counsel* version. The more secular language allowed me a way in and at last I was able to respond to God's 'tricks' and to begin the long, slow journey towards love and trust, as my relationship with God moved from being non-existent (at any conscious level) to the most important and central one in my life.

But it needed one further trick for this to become the case. A trick which ensured that I went to a place where God could approach me so directly that my life would be changed forever. In the February of 1994 I went to a Clerk's course at Woodbrooke, the Quaker Study Centre in Birmingham, where I heard about Responding to Conflict, a course on international mediation and conflict resolution. I was already familiar with neighbourhood mediation and in a small way undertook mediation within my work environment, and I felt drawn to working in this area more widely, but I was hesitant. I felt

I needed time to discern whether this was the right path for me. To that end I had a small, impromptu clearness meeting from which I concluded that this could be an area to which I was being called, and if so 'way would open'. It did, and in January 1995 I returned to Woodbrooke.

A spiritual tornado

I arrived confident that I knew exactly what I was doing there, and what I was going to do with the rest of my life, but within three weeks, just long enough for me to have made good connections with some fellow Quakers, I found myself completely blown 'off course'. I had prayed to give myself up to God, and now God was calling me on my prayer. I had a series of dreams, both waking and sleeping, over a period of some eight weeks which essentially revealed to me that everything I had thought myself to be was a sham. It sounds so mild phrased that way, but it was horrifying to see myself truly. The phrase used by early Friends, 'being broken open', exactly describes it, and it is every bit as painful as the words imply. I was fortunate to have available to me experienced and skilled guidance, without which my confused and frightened state might well have over-whelmed me.

The next couple of months were exhausting. This was no small nudging from God. I was immersed in an experience which com-pletely unravelled my sense of who I was, the person I believed myself to be, the way in which I was living, the masks behind which I operated... everything I thought I knew was obliterated. I was a vast great empty space, a nothingness; and it was terrifying. So far as I am concerned the Hebrew scriptures are right. One cannot see God and live (Exodus 33: 20). Just to be caught up in the vortex of the wind of the Holy Spirit is enough for me, and as close as I want to get in this life.

There is absolutely no way I would knowingly have entered into such an experience. Did God know this? Is that why I found it being made possible for me to go for a significant period of time to Woodbrooke for apparently utilitarian reasons? I felt then, and on the whole feel today, that God tricked me into being in a place where I could be reached, where my natural defences were lower than usual, where I felt safe and could afford to be more vulnerable than normal. I think I had what is sometimes described as a 'spiritual emergency'. Was it luck that there was a particular confluence of people at Woodbrooke that term? Does God actually intervene in such very concrete ways in our lives? Or was it because of that confluence that I was able to allow my real feelings to surface and be faced? Is God always searching for us, always seeking our attention and our willingness to listen, so that when we are in a place where this can happen, where we can allow it to happen, God can sweep us up and take us into a different dimension altogether?

I don't know. I only know that what I experienced turned my life upside down. From knowing precisely what I was going to do for the foreseeable future I found myself living with a level of unknowing that was beyond anything I had ever experienced. I suddenly understood 'experimentally' what early Friends described, and found George Fox's advice – to look towards the Light as the only way out of the morass in which truly seeing ourselves pitches us – to be as relevant today as it was in the mid 1600s. I found myself called to live in a completely different manner; to discover who God desired me to be; what it was God wanted me to do. Intellectually I can recognise that this was a choice. Spiritually and emotionally, however, there never seemed any choice.

It is difficult to describe living without landmarks, without reference points by which to locate oneself. I felt lost in a very real way, and focused all my energy on trying to understand and make sense of what was happening to me. I understood that I was being called to learn what it is to live lovingly. I understood that God was saying to me that if I really meant what I had prayed for, then it was time for me to take up the task of learning what it is really to love, to love as we are told Jesus loved – without fear and totally present for the other. To do this I must learn to put aside my egocentricity, my need to be in control, my mistrustfulness and my pretences. To do this I must be willing to be vulnerable, open, accepting and unmasked. To do this I must know myself as God knows me, and I understood that this was going to be very difficult for me. What I *didn't* understand was why God seemed to be making a hard task even harder by seemingly calling me to be open to the idea of living in a committed relationship with a man.

There were so many very good reasons why this was ridiculous. To begin with I had been celibate for years. I had made the decision some ten years before that it wasn't possible to live in true partnership with a man. Not only was I incapable of true intimacy, but so were men. In terms of companionship and friendship I preferred women, and the network of friendships which undergirded my life consisted primarily of women, some gay men and a few ex-lovers. I had never found it possible to have uncomplicated friendship with heterosexual men and rarely found I liked them enough to want to. Then there was the fact that in my late 40s, any men I might meet were extremely unlikely to be free and available; and less likely even than this, was that they would desire the kind of intentional, mindful, God-centred partnership that I felt was being required of me. What kind of a trick was God playing on me? At this point I echoed Hadewijch of Brabant (where Love = God):

> Sweet as Love's nature is,
> Where can she come by the strange hatred
> With which she continually pursues me
> And transpierces the depths of my heart with storm?
> I wander in darkness without clarity,
> Without liberating consolation, and in strange fear.
> ... It is plain that Love has dealt with me deceitfully.
> (Hart 1980: 229)

It felt to me as if it was the single most impossible thing that could have been asked of me. Never mind the extreme practical improbabilities, I didn't *want* to do this. In fact it was arguably the

very last thing in the world I wanted. Allistair Lomax in an article in
The Friend wrote:

> I am inevitably led to ponder about what I would be
> prepared to give up for the love of Christ ... We do not
> know when he will ask us or what will be required of us,
> we can only hope that, when the crunch comes, we will
> be ready ... (Lomax 1998: 11).

Well I wasn't. I wasn't ready to give up my prejudices about men.
I wasn't ready to entertain the possibility of a committed permanent
relationship. I wasn't ready to give up the freedom that being single
allowed me. I wasn't ready for the intimacy that being in such a relationship required. Most importantly I wasn't ready for the change
that was being asked of me. But ready or not, changed I was.

A new place – a changed life

Had there been opportunities for this change to have happened
before? Had I been offered continuously the possibility of realising
that union with another person is linked with union with God? Was
that what God's tricks and tests had been about over so many years?
If what we read in the Bible is truthful, then God never gives up on
us, so the answer probably has to be 'Yes'. After all, God must try
and reach us as we are, where we are, however unpromising that
appears to be. Whether God uses serial tricks (one building on
another, each timed for maximum effectiveness), or is just persistent,
is a question I have not yet come to any conclusions about.

It would seem that my very focused, task oriented, tightly constructed way of living in the material world was a bulwark between
me and the deep spiritual truth I was confronted with at Woodbrooke, but at the time I was unaware that this was how I lived. It
wasn't until God had stripped away my illusions about my 'self' that
I could begin to appreciate the extent of the barriers I had constructed and why it was so extraordinarily difficult for me to find
myself in a state of total unknowingness about my future. Always in

the past, no matter what was happening in my life, I was able to look ahead, see what the various choices were, and, of those, which ones were really available to me. I had a sense of reality, so I didn't set myself impossible tasks and I enjoyed the continual movement and adventurousness of my life. None of this was true any more. It wasn't that I didn't want to continue to live in this way. It was just that it simply wasn't possible any longer. My inner landscape had been irrevocably changed.

The only thing I was certain of was that I didn't know what I was going to be doing. I pushed aside the extraordinary idea that I was to open myself up to the possibility of a committed relationship. No. There had to be something more sensible, practical, concrete, attainable, towards which all this was leading me. But I had no sense of it at all. In fact the only sense I had was that I shouldn't return to full-time work immediately. I was deeply suspicious of that; how very convenient for me.

Was I just being work-shy? That seemed improbable, given my previous work history, but I couldn't be sure. I had a clearness meeting which was useful, in that I had to formulate clearly where I was, but it helped me not at all in discerning where I was going to. I remained in a thick fog and felt completely helpless, a state that causes me acute discomfort at the best of times, and in these circumstances bordered on the unbearable. The confusion, bewilderment, and occasional moments of panic were things I slowly realised I was going to have to learn to live with. None of it was made easier by the puzzled questions from other friends, particularly my secular friends, who not only didn't recognise this 'I haven't a clue what I'm going to do' Gay, but who felt such an attitude was somehow improper and feckless (a judgment I could well understand).

This wasn't the only total change. I had previously never been lonely. I really didn't know what it was. I had often been puzzled when people spoke of being lonely, and assumed they confused being alone with loneliness. I'm not saying I hadn't had moments of feeling isolated, outside of a social group, separate from others. That sort of relatively momentary loneliness I knew quite well. What I had never encountered before was a deep, bottomless loneliness, that sense of an inner void that is unfillable, unexplainable, and is the reality in which we all dwell. All our contacts with others, all our activities, all our relationships, love affairs, friendships, work, play, whatever, screen this Truth, and may even be the way we attempt to fill the void, and almost certainly seek to avoid awareness of it. Perhaps that is why people seem to confuse being alone with loneliness. Perhaps it isn't a confusion after all, since being alone may confront us with ourselves, and once that happens avoiding knowledge of the void is very difficult.

What happened for me was that I could no longer screen the void. It now lived consciously in my everyday existence. It still does. I continue to do and enjoy the things I've always done and enjoyed, and most of the time I still find life good, interesting, stimulating and even exciting. But nothing masks the void. I am accompanied by loneliness. I have discovered over the last few years that I am not alone in this, and many great spiritual guides have written and spoken of it in ways that I find helpful and illuminating. One at least believes that our loneliness is God's loneliness, and I find that oddly comforting. I have glimmerings of the truth that accepting this loneliness, learning to live from within the void, is what living in the heart of God is all about, but that doesn't stop me from feeling intermittently extremely angry with God, exclaiming 'I was quite happy *not* knowing what loneliness was, thank you very much!'

There have been other changes too, changes which have caused seismic shifts in my attitude towards others and life generally; changes brought about by the compelling call to 'wake up' and come alive to the reality of God's love, and to live that love out in the world. I realised quite young that we cannot possess or own others, but I used this knowledge as a defence against real loving and intimacy. I saw it not as a spiritual truth with gifts, but as a hard fact of life. It was this, as much as anything else, which made me determinedly uncommitted. I chose to trust only myself, thereby separating myself from others. I chose to live defensively rather than freely, believing I was doing the latter. I mistook isolation for security, a mistake as great as that of thinking security lies in possession and ownership. Vaguely I knew my lovelessness, but I chose to ignore it, a choice which is no longer available to me.

It seems to me that what the trail shows me is that throughout my life there have been two constants. God was constantly present, constantly seeking my attention, constantly being presented to me; and so was love, God's love mediated to me through others. My father who showed me what it was to love freely and gaily; missionary friends who showed me what it was to love selflessly and passionately; yet others who showed me what it was to love wholeheartedly and faithfully; and good friends who continue to show me what it is to love honestly and tolerantly. All this I have learned from, valued and cherished, but I have never learned what it is to love another with the kind of intimacy which opens us to union with God. That would have been to risk exposure of what and who I really am – to make myself vulnerable to the point of annihilation. Yet I think that this is what we are all called to do. To love others as God loves us requires this of us, and requires this of us consciously. Thus I have come to understand why I felt God was calling me into committed relationship with a man. God is closest when we are lovingly intimate with another. This does not have to include sexual intimacy, but for those of us who have great difficulty in giving ourselves up, in allowing ourselves to be open to dissolving in God, then the sexual encounter is one of the places where the ability to do this can be discovered. For me to open myself to this possibility is a change beyond anything I ever imagined.

My life choices have finally brought me to a place, both physically and spiritually, where I can be broken open to this knowledge by God and changed by it. Perhaps I could have arrived here sooner, or more easily, but I suspect the journey I took was necessary for me and that in some deep recess of my soul I knew that. Some seeds have very hard shells, and need to be buried and frozen for a long period before they are ready to burst into Life.

Conclusion

I spoke at the beginning of the tension I experience in believing simultaneously in an interventionist and a non-interventionist God. No less of a tension is the fact that alongside my passionate belief in God, lie my doubts, uncertainties and occasional downright *dis*belief. I am essentially a rationalist. For years I didn't believe life was anything more than an accident: that there was no purpose or meaning to it other than that which we created. The struggle to understand what it is for struck me as pointless. We know nothing lasts. We know nothing endures. So we seek to have fun and enjoy ourselves while we can. This often has a frantic quality to it as we race against time, fearful of our mortality, living always in the shadow of that knowledge and trying to avoid it at all costs. We seek peace, harmony, serenity, and happiness continuously – sometimes through questionable and often directly self-defeating means, e.g. alcohol, which is actually a depressant, yet people drink because they feel miserable or down. I always regarded believing in God as just one of a variety of ways of making sense of life. Part of me grieves that this is no longer true for me. It is so much easier to believe that nothing matters really.

I have become aware as I look back over my life for God's action in it, that in fact God has always been present, always available to me. The trouble was that with my father's death the only theology readily available provided me with the kind of antediluvian authority figure that was utterly objectionable to me. There was nothing appealing about the after-life, and indeed if it proved to be true, there would be nobody I valued or wanted to spend time with in 'heaven' anyway! Furthermore there seemed to be considerable confusion and contradiction in this God. On the one hand He is all-loving, all-compassionate, and so forth, and on the other if you don't do what He tells you, you will be punished – probably in this life, and if not, then definitely in the next one. When I asked questions, there appeared to be all sorts of weaselly ways to explain and justify this, most of which disgusted me and none of which was believable. There was nothing attractive, appealing or compelling about God at all. It took me years to realise that the God so described was simply a human interpretation – and I might say fantasy, for who really 'knows' what God is or isn't?

I think now, that there was always a part of me which knew God was real. A part of me which recognised and engaged with God in others, however unwittingly and unknowingly. I wrote earlier of the tension I feel between a transcendent and an immanent God. An 'external' God who moves mountains and causes things to happen, and an 'internal' God who is the still small voice which prompts, urges, guides, admonishes and calls us into Life.

I have deliberately not described my transcendent God as omnipotent. To believe that would be to believe horrors such as the Holocaust, the Killing Fields of Pol Pot, the massacres in Rwanda could be prevented by God. Such a theology takes me perilously close to the God of my childhood, a God I would reject even if real. I hold a theology close to that of Henri Nouwen, Thomas Merton, Julian of Norwich, St Benedict. Here there is a transcendent God who is a true creator. Having made a thing and given it life, it must be left free. In our case this means to be free to make our own choices, our own decisions; and this is where, for me at least, the immanent God comes in, the part of God that breathes life into us. *Ruach*, God's breath, lives within us, is part of our Being, speaks to us and connects us intimately with each other, the whole of the cosmos and the transcendent God.

As I learn to practise a spiritual discipline, to be obedient, to surrender to God's love, my life seems to be expanding. My fears seem to be diminishing (or at least my fear of being overwhelmed by my fears), my anxieties and concerns about the future disappearing. My capacity to live, my ability to love and be loved, my willingness to trust, to be vulnerable and open to others, my capacity for intimacy

– all these are slowly emerging, developing and growing stronger. My life has a richness, a fullness, a wonder-fulness unimaginable to me previously.

Intellectually, rationally, I still believe that life is chaotic and arbitrary, that things happen randomly and without purpose. Experientially however, I know that if I am open to it, if I look to the Light, if I invite God into my seeing, if I am obedient and listen to God, my perspective is completely altered. That is not to say that things will suddenly become as I want them to be. The *facts* of my life are not altered, but the way I perceive them is, and this provides me with opportunities for living in ways otherwise unavailable to me. Thus I can choose to see what has happened to me in my life as God playing tricks on me, or I can choose to see God testing me, or I can choose to see God inviting me and calling me. Or... I can choose to see God inviting and calling me through tricking and testing me! On balance this *is* how I understand it. If indeed God tricked me into being where I now find myself, then I cannot be anything but glad.

References

Frost, R. *The Poetry of Robert Frost: The Collected Poems*. New York: Henry Holt & Co, 1979.

Guenther, M. *Holy Listening: The Art of Spiritual Direction*. London: Darton, Longman & Todd, 1996.

Hart, C. *Hadewijch: The Complete Works*. New York: Paulist Press, 1980.

Lomax, A. 'Reflections'. In *The Friend*, 6 March 1998: 11.

Nouwen, H. *The Return of the Prodigal Son: A Story of Homecoming*. London: Darton, Longman & Todd, 1994.

The Grail Psalms (Singing Version). Glasgow: William Collins Sons & Co, 1990.

The Belly of the Whale

Margery Post Abbott

The Lord God appointed a bush, and made it come up over Jonah, to give shade over his head, to save him from his discomfort; so Jonah was very happy about the bush. But when dawn came up the next day, God appointed a worm that attacked the bush, so that it withered. When the sun rose, God prepared a sultry east wind, and the sun beat down on the head of Jonah, so that he was faint and asked that he might die. He said, 'It is better for me to die than to live' (Jonah 4: 6-8).

What kind of God creates beauty and peace in an instant, then takes it away? What kind of God uses creation to torment humanity? Arbitrary, capricious and distant. That is how God seems at times – especially the distant part. It seems particularly perverse for God to pay attention to one man in order to torment him. After all, God had just driven Jonah into the belly of a whale, then relented only after three days, and allowed the fish to spit him onto the shore. If anyone had a complaint against God, Jonah did!

So why does Jonah speak to me? I am selective about how I read the Bible. I find words which tell me of the state of my soul and my relationship with God. They roll around inside me for weeks or years. The words become my own.

> I feel little impulse to read systematically
> in the Bible or to study the history
> of the peoples of the Bible.
>> But phrases catch me.
> The words speak to me. Here. Now. Fresh.
> I cannot know what they meant two thousand,
> or even three thousand years ago. I respond now.
> Play them into my computer.
> Read them in multiple translations.
>> Always aware they are translations.
> I know no Greek, Aramaic or Hebrew.
>> Always translations of translations –
> of language and of culture. The words carry meaning
> when they touch my soul. Free-floating of the meaning
> they once carried (or are they?)
>> Grounded in the history of generations.

So this short story of miracles and torment comes to be on my table. 'Jonah saved from the belly of the whale!' is one headline for this story. But the same entity who saved him, put him there. 'Huge vine grows overnight to shade man sitting in the desert!' is another splashy offer of consolation. But the next night an equally ambitious and unlikely worm cuts it down.

> God, do you play with us so?
> What purposes could justify such a God?

Thinking about the title of this book, *God the Trickster?*, I ask these questions. But sitting with Jonah, I have no questions. Reading about Jonah, I encounter a theologian who asserts that Jonah is 'a short parable characterized by fantastic events to poke fun indirectly at a little man whose inner thoughts remain virtually hidden' (Crenshaw 1993: 380-1). This theologian's perspective admits nothing of the power of hatred. Jonah spills out his motives. His inner reactions drive the plot. No worthwhile theology can ignore the strength of human purpose and the inertia of weights in the heart. While the fantastic actions of the great fish have delighted children for centuries, the swallowing also evokes an inner darkness which needs no further explanation for those who have known it.

The answer is not about God's purposes, but about the stubbornness and hard-headedness of humanity – this I feel with every bone of my soul. Every time I see great beauty and look away, each time I shrug off a proffered hand of comfort, I can see more clearly how I cherish my own way of doing things. I cherish old ways even when logic, my heart and soul all tell me this old behavior is not what I truly want. It is no surprise that God has to take drastic steps to get my attention.

I also know Jonah's story is an inward one. A story of dangerous anger against what he loves most. An anger grounded in hatred of a city which is the enemy of his people. An anger which turns inward and eats at him as he tries to hide. An anger which turns to depression which swallows him up in its dank inertia.

Even when freed from the confinement of the belly and having acted as God required, Jonah continues to revel in his anger. Hatred remains the purpose of his life. Nothing but a persistent and inventive God can change this. We do not see the end, do not know more about Jonah's life. But the abrupt ending tells us of the choice. The fact that his story survives implies Jonah's response.

This story of faith and torment comes at a fortuitous moment for me. I am ready to look afresh at my relationships with those around me and with God. I am ready to let go of my anger but don't know how to do it. So this meditation on Jonah is an unfinished story, a gift with unknown consequences.

✸

And the Lord said, 'Is it right for you to be angry?' Then
Jonah went out of the city and sat down east of the city,
and made a booth for himself there. He sat under it in the
shade, waiting to see what would become of the city (Jonah
4: 4, 5).

A sparrow just came and landed feet first on the small feeder
the finches use. This sparrow did not stay, eating little of the food.
But it chased the finches off. After it left, the finches returned and
enthusiastically, if warily, munched away. One finch, on guard, lifts
its head and checks with every bite. The other seems more trusting
and eats awhile, then looks.

How often my outbursts seem like the action of that sparrow. I
lash out. I feel like the world is against me. Nothing I want to see
happen does. My desire for revenge, for hurt, for striking out is real
but often without real object. Yet – and this is part of the change – I
see that this is not the motive of the sparrow. Is it really mine?

I lie down on my back at the end of yoga class. The teacher tells
us to relax, to press our backs into the floor, to feel it lift us, to let go
of all the stresses of the day. I wait with trepidation, wondering at my
increasing anxiety. The sensation is so strong that something is about
to land on me, to cause me to double up in pain. A feeling as old as
the cradle.

Anger and depression are so close. Flight is such a natural reflex.
Jonah sought to flee to Tarshish when the Lord God asked more
than he was willing to give. He fled and entered into the belly of the
whale – wallowed in the deep dankness of the inner dark.

> That place was my home for so long I do not recall what
> I was fleeing.
> I cannot claim to flee God, cannot claim to know God
> in my running.
> Yet I can see myself, sitting outback in the night as a child.
> Longing. Dreaming without dreams.
> In wonderment at the immensity and mystery of the
> universe.

Another night, inwardly screaming at this bearded old
      mental image of a God who failed me.
Rejecting him and all he stood for.
Yet again, flailing at the sticky sweetness of a picture.
The long, sandy hair and white robes of this man
standing there with a lamb did not reassure me.
            Impotence is all I caught.
No capacity to bring what I needed in my soul.
Incredible fury welled up, unallowed.

How much was my rejection of Christ's comfort responsible for
pitching me overboard into the fish's belly? For so long, I claimed
my life as my doing, my responsibility. I took pride in my own ability
to control my actions: took responsibility for cause and effect. At
some level I labeled Jesus as impotent and God as far removed. I was
irrelevant to 'His' schemes: He was so abstract that no schemes were
possible. I left God blended into the infinite background to the
world even as I longed to know the Infinite. I did not deny 'Him', I
just did not believe 'He' had any relation to me, any awareness of me.
My life was mine to live, mine to destroy.

Did God call out to me as a child, ask me to forgive? To be an
agent of forgiveness and healing to those who had hurt me? To
prophesy? I have no memory of such words. I did not consider the
possibility of such a call, of any 'call' for that matter. That stuff was
all too weird! Off the radar screen! Yet looking back I can see that
God was never far from hand. That much I know now.

Pink flowered wallpaper and the matching painted twin beds were
the setting of so many encounters. I was pleased to claim my sister's
room during her college days even though I hated pink. It was there
that I argued with the patriarchal God and rejected the Sunday
School images of Jesus. It was there that I knew God was more than
I had been taught. The balcony of that room held a riot of wisteria in
the spring. It sat surrounded by tall oaks and maples with a window
to the hope-filled stars. The trellis offered me a tenuous escape to the
garden and the path into the freedom and comfort of the woods.

The cream-colored vanity was trimmed in a dusky pink. I can still see myself, sitting on the woven bench and looking in that triple mirror – disliking what I saw on the surface. Yet I found myself defiant. Attempts to make myself more like the popular girls with lip colors and mascara became sour, trite, and then ended. It was my declaration that anyone who was going to be my friend would have to take me as I was. Loneliness was a cherished friend. I did much to keep it near, yet there was also a precious truth, a kernel of myself, that I was desperate to hold on to, no matter what the cost.

At night lights had to be out by ten o'clock sharp and books put away. So I gathered my flashlight, first a full-sized one, then a series of pencil-sized variety so no light would betray me under the door. Under the covers I could get away with more. Read a bunch of the Bible that way. Somehow compelled to read it from cover to cover. Once my mind was made up, I did a lot of strange things.

None of my paints and few of my dolls came with me from my old small space to that many-windowed pink room. It was not a place for such things. My collection of books stayed as well in the tiny room that always was somehow mine. This room with all its space and conventions of beauty never really belonged to me or I to it. I held tight the solitude and fear I knew best. Whatever voice I heard, I could not bring myself to trust.

Those same years, growing up in a Quaker family, I felt the power of the silence in worship on First and Fourth Day mornings. Being in that big old meetinghouse with high ceilings and huge, tall windows still evokes a sense of peace. The light played through the room in constant variation. Odd noises punctuated the light. Games played through my head as I imagined the lives and motives of those around me. Delight alternated with times of boredom and itchiness. I cringed at Dr McMann's sermons. I cringed even more at a cousin standing and talking about the sacredness of all life. She could not harm even an insect. I could never be that mushy!

✦

> *The waters closed in over me; deep surrounded me; weeds*
> *were wrapped around my head at the roots of the mountains*
> (Jonah 2: 5).

I ran. I hid where I thought I could never be found. I ran from the pain and from a concept of brotherly love which smothered me. I ran inward where no one could find me or hurt me. I knew I wasn't a 'stupid gi-irl!' I knew I could do it all as well as they could. I measured myself by objective measures. Opinions, tears, delight, were dangerous. I did not believe the words of my mouth unless they could be proven. I had no words for emotion or faith. Algebraic equations suited me just fine. Test tubes promised the certainty and verification I desired above all. Inside books, the pain was less.

> In the belly of the whale, the world is finite and warm.
> You can fight and thrash and punch all you want
> and all you meet is yielding resistance.
>   Nothing else exists.
> The anger feeds on the warm waters and half-digested kill,
> but touches only you. In the belly of the whale,
> the world is distant. Naught exists but you
> and the center of creation. In the belly of the whale
> you consume yourself or you give yourself to your
>   Creator.
> You can live a long time in the belly of the whale.

Does the lesson of Jonah apply to the anger of a small child, carried in the heart well beyond all reason or purpose?

Science offered a safe perspective from which to hunt out the secrets of the universe. I was fascinated by its tools. While at college, a gentle, brilliant, quiet man came into my life. Married, we moved away, seeking our own place in the world. In Chicago, then Indiana, I thrived in the lab. Then this dream collapsed. Finding a way became tentative. The years accumulated.

✵

Then the Lord spoke to the fish, and it spewed Jonah out
upon the dry land (Jonah 2: 10).

Coming out on shore is only the first step. Several years ago, when I was sojourning at Woodbrooke, I became part of a small group exploring prayer. One day we took large sheets of paper and each drew our lifelines. On the paper we explored times of closeness to God and times of distance. We mapped our connections to our religious communities in a similar way. These two drawings played off each other in a way I could not ignore. Without engagement in a faith community, God was not in my awareness. Only in the face of death and the solace of worship did my defenses drop enough to experience the all-encompassing love of God and hear the call to change my life.

Even as I accepted that call, I fought it and sought to run away in what I can only guess was a repeat of my childhood response. But once I knew that Voice, I found myself engaged. God drew me out of my isolation. A child who hated poetry, I found myself, forty years later, writing reams. A person terrified of talking, even to friends, I was called to speak. A lover of science and technology, I was called to write of matters of the soul. A woman prone to darkness, I now find myself pushed to know laughter.

❖

'What is your occupation? Where do you come from? What
is your country? And of what people are you?' 'I am a
Hebrew,' he replied. 'I worship the Lord, the God of heaven,
who made the sea and the dry land' (Jonah 1: 8, 9).

Sometimes, when I am asked that inevitable question 'How did you find Friends?', I speak of the multiple times I have come to Friends. At first it was passive. I happened to be born into a Quaker family. Not much choice about that! As I grew, I began to find my own way. I came to love the silence of worship.

Next, the stories of those who committed their lives to what they believed reached out to me. With other teenage Friends, I listened with awe as a teacher spoke of his years in the penitentiary. He had refused to register for the draft during the Korean War. So I found Quakerism anew in my college years by protesting the war in Vietnam and tutoring poor children – actions which made my Republican parents uneasy.

As a young married woman, I started to find social connections as I made friends those few years we had a Meeting community in Chicago. This period was also my first awareness of the wider Quaker world when I was shocked to discover a Friends church, complete with pastor, nearby. Too quickly came the unconnected years when I gave up my dream of doing doctoral work in chemistry. I thrashed to find another direction. The women's movement gave me purpose, a legacy of childhood tales about Lucretia Mott melded with the resistance I faced in wanting to be a scientist. Tales of the actions of Quakers in the past helped shape my actions.

We were scarcely settled in Portland, Oregon, before my husband and I got pulled in to an active Meeting and started to engage our faith in a new way. The former factory building with its small door and long dark entrance hall were deceptive. The meeting room was dark, the carpet an ugly yellow, the neighbor determined to make himself known by running his power mower at 10.00 a.m. on Sundays. Friends there made it clear we were welcome, with invitations to dinner. They made it clear we were needed, with rapid requests from Nominating Committee. The connections were right. We were hooked. Multnomah Monthly Meeting is still our spiritual home twenty years later.

In Portland, something slowly took hold of me. Entering into the work of the Meeting, I learned much about the practical efforts it takes to keep a community connected and make it a welcoming place. I thrived on remodeling the Meeting House and managing the property. Worship was important, somehow, but it was mainly a time of quiet for me, a time to reflect on the week and to catch my breath between diving into projects and the demands of a high-pressure job. So each time I came to Friends, I found something new, but for most of my life this something has been expressed and experienced in practical doing.

Only after the Meeting asked me to be its Clerk, did I start to learn about another dimension of listening. The Meeting was being torn apart by the intensity of feelings around marrying lesbian and gay couples. Sitting at the table on one edge of the circle for those two years taught me much. Simple necessity forced me to explore my heritage with fresh eyes. A new sense of being part of the Religious Society of Friends as I sought to be open to ways through all the pain and anger around me. I also sought that something more which I could only find in the listening but had no words to express. The intense listening beyond words is one of the gifts to me from those two years as Clerk. Another gift was the surprise of trust, the surprise that the Meeting would trust me in this way and, at times, even listen to me. The loneliness and walls created by anger eased once more.

❂

The Lord God appointed a bush, and made it come up over Jonah, to give shade over his head, to save him from his discomfort; so Jonah was very happy about the bush (Jonah 4: 6).

Hearing the voice of God. Being permeated by light and joy all mingled in with grief and tears. Knowing safety in the arms of God as a solitary soul. Hearing through the ears of God words directed to the silence, piercing the darkness of my heart. 'O come, O come, Emanuel, and ransom captive Israel. Who stands in lonely exile here, until the son of man appear. Rejoice! Rejoice! Emanuel, will ransom captive Israel.' Words from this hymn and vocal ministry, tears, love, and grief all flowed through the Meeting for Worship in Gwynedd,

Pennsylvania, near where my father had just died. In the worship I knew Dad was with the God he loved so well.

At Gwynedd Meeting House a friend was sitting on the facing bench. She was embarrassed at the meeting that morning, so overfilled with words. She almost forced me to stand and introduce myself at the end of worship, then saw the tears and stopped. In the worship, a woman had spoken of encountering ducks on the road. An old man rambled incoherently. They and others called me to love and compassion. All blended as an opening to my life: a new stage of my life where my heart could be broken open and my soul made visible. In that worship came a call to ministry, a call for me to speak of the workings of God in my heart. A strange call for one so buried in the silence. For one so deeply embedded in the belly of the whale.

In the call to ministry were also gentle instructions to find support for examining my emotional life and my spiritual life. Learn to be present to the community. I was no longer alone. Trust the Spirit – trust the intuitive response that is deeper than the reflexive. Learn to keep my rational self in balance with my heart and soul.

Others must accompany me on this path. It was not to be trod alone. The memory of anger and the pull of the darkness were too strong. I could not learn to trust my heart – to trust God is more the point – travelling solo. Yet I learned I had to honor the past even as I set it aside.

✵

> But when dawn came up the next day, God appointed a worm that attacked the bush, so that it withered. When the sun rose, God prepared a sultry east wind, and the sun beat down on the head of Jonah, so that he was faint and asked that he might die. He said, 'It is better for me to die than to live' (Jonah 4: 7, 8).

Much of the time I really don't want to change. These past months and years, it amazes me how often I will do anything rather than pray or sit at the computer and write. When my mood is bright, I can laugh at other days when the appeal of mopping the kitchen floor well outweighs the discomfort of what I am called to do. Some days, I would rather do most anything than the work God has called me to perform. I watch and wait for something spectacular to happen to relieve me of the consequences. I want to be relieved of doing more.

When I do delve into my work, I love doing it. When I think about it, I am angry and afraid. The prospect is too much for me. I cling to my image of myself as a recluse. I want to confirm my belief that I have nothing to say worth saying. I would rather re-enter the belly of the fish than do what God has called me to do.

Each time I prepare to lead a retreat, to teach a class, to speak the words I am given, I resist. The worm starts chewing at my shelter. But something holds me fast. Once I have made the commitment, I do follow through. In the process of the doing, I know the joy which brought me there. If I mention my trepidation to participants, someone inevitably speaks to the light in my eye and the love which is present.

✵

But God said to Jonah, 'Is it right for you to be angry about the bush?' And he said, 'Yes, angry enough to die.' Then the Lord said, 'You are concerned about the bush, for which you did not labor and which you did not grow; it came into being in a night, and perished in a night. And should I not be concerned about Nineveh, that great city, in which there are more than a hundred and twenty thousand persons who do not know their right hand from their left, and also many animals?' (Jonah 4: 9-11).

Recently, a small group gathered for prayer at my house. We used the form of prayer established by St Ignatius where participants place themselves imaginatively into a Bible passage. They are asked to focus on the phrase or verse which catches at them. We listened as the story from Luke of Jesus' temptation in the desert was read in several versions. I was immediately standing on the parapet of the temple in Jerusalem. The stones were harsh, yet comforting to my hand. The sky was deep blue and the hills in sharp array around the city. I felt great pleasure in looking across the valley.

I was also reluctantly aware of the words 'Thou shalt not tempt the Lord thy God'. In *The Message* (a paraphrase of the Bible), Jesus was more direct in stating: 'Beat it, Satan!' (Matt. 4: 10). I suddenly saw how I had been sitting back and daring God to make the book I was called to write – and so much else in my life – happen. I had been avoiding work, hoping to prove God wrong in some way, daring God to rescue this project if it were really so valuable. I was sitting back in my chair, cursing the hot winds, hoping God would not rescue Nineveh. Hoping God would rescue Nineveh. But I sure wasn't going to cooperate any more than I had to.

❂

> *But this was very displeasing to Jonah, and he became angry. He prayed to the Lord and said, 'O Lord! Is not this what I said while I was still in my own country? That is why I fled to Tarshish at the beginning; for I knew that you are a gracious God and merciful, slow to anger and abounding in steadfast love, and ready to relent from punishing. And now, O Lord, please take my life from me, for it is better for me to die than to live.' And the Lord said, 'Is it right for you to be angry?'* (Jonah 4: 1-4).

'I know you are a gracious God and merciful, slow to anger and abounding in steadfast love.' 'That is why I fled.' Anger and bitterness have a life of their own. They become companions on the way. I do not know how to proceed without them. They formed me. Do not ask me to abandon them. It is a righteous anger which I feel against those who have harmed me. I can show this to the world, offer proof of their ill-doing. Is it not right that I hate them who demonstrate their hate for You by harming those whom You love?

> Yet You pursued Jonah. You did not give up on him.
> You followed as he fled to the ends of the earth.
> You used a storm to shake him as
> he hid in the bowels of the ship.
> You sought to reach him through the suffering crew
> yet, still, he asked to be thrown into the sea
> and was swallowed up by a fish.
> You stayed with him through it all
>   – through the anger, the fear and the depression –
> places he thought you would not/could not follow.
> You desired that he know of love
> and act out your love towards his enemies.

Through this all Jonah was steadfast in his faith. He believed above all that You were merciful. He fled in fear of God – not because You were about to destroy him, but because of his own sin. He knew that he was not righteous and loving in Your eyes. He did not believe he could change and be what You asked him to be. I know this. How often have I done the same without even recognizing the ways in which I flee You. Now I see a life-long pattern. Now I am sitting outside Nineveh hoping above hope that it will still be destroyed and I can continue in my righteousness. I want them to live up to my expectations of my enemy. I want God to intervene with fury. I want to see the fireworks of retribution. So I sit in my chair and watch, angry that I have done as much as I have done.

> Times, you fill my heart with joy.
>   You offer me words to share what is on my heart.
>   You offer me comfort and love.
> You make me aware of all that is wondrous in this world.
> You seem to respond to every prayer.

Jonah could not bear to save the 120,000 men, women and children of Nineveh and all their animals. I am not sure what I am called to save, only that I am called to speak of God and the ways I have come to know God. I am called into the depths of my soul and to share what I find there. What the consequences are I do not know.

❂

> *I went down to the land whose bars closed upon me forever; yet you brought up my life from the Pit, O Lord my God* (Jonah 2: 6).

Lucretia Mott spoke often of cooperating, co-creating, with God. Whatever God has in store for us and for this world, it will not happen against our will and without our actions. It has been said that the Garden of Eden is an attempt to explain free will in the face of an omnipotent God. God asks, God suggests, God tells us what we need to know in order for us to live in the paradise this world might be. But we are filled with too much curiosity, and too much desire to control our own futures, to be willing to listen to God's word passively. We want the fruit of knowledge. The price of that fruit is to live our lives more under our own desires than in accord with our Creator.

Stopping, listening, and paying attention to the guidance that is there for us, brings us back towards the Garden. Being open to the mystery that is Love lifts us out of the Pit. The 40th Psalm speaks to my heart:

> I waited patiently for the Lord;
> You inclined to me and heard my cry.
> You drew me up from the desolate pit,
> out of the miry bog,
> and set my feet upon a rock,
> making my steps secure.

I seem to be one who keeps tripping back into the bog. Knowing that the rock is really there helps me hang on. I need to be lifted again and again. But I also need to make my own way once my feet are back again on that rock. Thus I come to see an iterative process. The times of listening, prayer, or desperate crying out are intermingled with the times of moving forward, confident and clear.

I return to Jonah and to the worm. God created the worm to cut down the vine even as God created the vine to comfort Jonah. Thus the lesson is in the east winds as much as it is in the shade of the broad leaves. I tend to assume (want to believe?) that God is in the comfort and that all the discomfort is of human origin. I often claim all the discomfort as my fault. Is this one more lesson small girls learn only too well?

Jonah's decision to answer yes to God came out of the belly of the fish, not out of the clear skies and mediterranean breezes. It took a worm and a blast of hot wind to get his attention again. An iterative process. Not random. Not designed to destroy. Meant to teach. Meant to bring Jonah to understand in his gut the destructiveness of his hatred towards Nineveh. Meant to bring Jonah to cooperate with God out of his own free will. C.S. Lewis speaks to this after the death of his wife:

> Bridge-players tell me that there must be some money on the game 'or else people won't take it seriously.' Apparently it's like that. Your bid – for God or no God, for a good God or the Cosmic Sadist, for eternal life or nonentity – will not be serious if nothing much is staked on it. And you will never discover how serious it was until the stakes are raised horribly high; until you find that you are playing not for counters or for sixpences but for every penny you have in the world. Nothing less will shake a man – or at any rate a man like me – out of his merely verbal thinking and his merely notional beliefs. He has to be knocked silly before he comes to his senses. Only torture will bring out the truth. Only under torture does he discover it himself (Lewis 1961: 31).

I have not known torture other than the inward sort, all too often self-imposed. Only in the grief following the loss of a parent could God penetrate my inward hearing and gain an active voice in my heart. Only in grief could I first recognize the power of God's love and the impetus it gives for turning who I was into what might be. Rationality loses appeal in the presence of death.

Soon after my mother died I was in worship, again in the Philadelphia area three thousand miles from home. I was in a meeting filled with many strangers, just as I had been after Dad died. Again the power of compassion filled the room and I was caught up in an awful mix of joy and uncontrolled tears. Again, no kleenex! (More tricks?) Again the words cut through to my core. A woman with a young child spoke of 20 hours of difficult labor, then giving up and falling into her husband's arms, trusting him to carry her and lead her through what was another seven hours before their child was born. For her, this spoke of God's presence when our own strength is gone. Another spoke of the translation of the Lord's Prayer from the Aramaic:

> Help us let go, clear the space inside of busy forgetfulness, so the Name comes to live. Create your reign of unity now – through our fiery hearts and willing hands (Douglas-Klotz 1990: 16, 19).

A man spoke the words of the God of Israel:

> For a brief moment I abandoned you, but with great compassion I will gather you (Isa. 54: 7).

I am still learning the meaning of the call which came to me so vividly after my father's death. The voice of God rang as clear in my soul after Mother's dying, but the leading remains to take form. The immediate call is to delight, to know that 'Jubilate Deo' runs through me. The message is bound up with the message of the Cross. Knowing that the suffering and fear are present as a wavering baseline through life but that we are called to step free of their bounds. We are called to move freely in their presence guided by the Inward Voice.

After thoughts

Sitting with Jonah has taught me much. About myself. About God. About the humor of God and about the melding of pain and humor. On this last my learning is just beginning. But a door has been opened. God does take us places we would never go ourselves, if we will listen and respond. God as 'Trickster' can show us the limitations of our concepts of the world and our own potential. The process is both iterative and voluntary. We cannot guess what saying 'Yes' might mean.

To follow a leading of God, two preconditions are essential. One must first hear and recognize the voice of God in one's inner ear. Then, one must be willing to respond. The core of this essay has been a meditation on the work of God in my life as I sat with Jonah in prayer. Many years God worked on me beneath the threshold of awareness, so I can only guess when I ran in fear and when I might have heard that still small voice in my soul. Only in recent years have I felt this voice with my whole being. God has called me to engage the world with skills I did not think I had and did not know I wanted.

This essay caused me to reflect on the concept of God the Trickster, a term that was uncomfortable for me six months ago when I started this process. As I have learned about myself and about God the concept of the Trickster has grown in meaning. The process itself has taken me in surprising directions as I consider how God broke through my protective shell and opened my life into fresh areas of creativity and potential.

Jonah makes a great tale for children. Of the Bible stories, it perhaps comes closest to the Native American myths of the Trickster. Jonah could easily be told to folks gathered around a fire. It lends itself easily to being acted out and is full of humor and exaggeration. Extraordinary events fill the story. God continually plays tricks on

Jonah, creating storms and a great fish to swallow him, growing vines in a day and just as capriciously cutting them down. God acts in ways which seem to have little to do with Jonah's description of 'a gracious God and merciful, slow to anger, and abounding in steadfast love'.

Like the Trickster myths of the Winnebago Tribe of North America, this story is one of education and development of the conscience. Unlike the Winnebago stories, where the Trickster is foolish and has his conscience awakened, in Jonah, God is both the Trickster and the one who seeks to teach.

Just as the Trickster makes fun of the traditions and rituals of the tribe, Jonah is easy to read as a parody on the prophets of Israel. The disclaimers of inadequacy voiced by Moses, Isaiah and Jeremiah are here carried into a story of total flight to the ends of the earth. The hardships and humiliations of the prophets are blown up into wild tales of fish, vines and worms. God's constant threats to destroy all those who disobey him are turned on their heads as God seeks to save Nineveh while Jonah pouts in anger.

The longer I reflect on Jonah, the more I see the humor in his story and in my own – a quite surprising consequence. Initially, I dismissed this possibility. Now the humor brings alive the darkness in the belly of the whale and is intermingled in Jonah's very real anger. The play of humor and anger recalls the mix of joy and grief I experienced when those close to me have died. Both are real. The one informs the other.

Paul Radin notes that in the Winnebago Trickster myths, we reach a point

> where ordinary words and terms are indeed completely inadequate. Only symbols, only metaphors, can convey the meaning properly (Radin 1973: 138).

The story of Jonah is full of rich symbols which speak to my condition. It brings to mind the writings of John of the Cross (or more recently, Sandra Cronk) on the dark night of the soul. In the dark night, God works on our hearts. Out of the darkest periods of our lives comes profound learning. Out of our stubborn natures come multiple times of learning. Jonah encountered, as have I, a God who is always present, even to the ends of the earth: a God who wants us to learn compassion for the whole world.

References

Crenshaw, J.L. 'The Book of Jonah'. In Metzger, B.M., and Coogan, M.D., eds., *The Oxford Companion to the Bible*. Oxford and New York: Oxford University Press, 1993: 380-81.

Cronk, S. *Dark Night Journey*. Wallingford, Pennsylvania: Pendle Hill Press, 1991.

Douglas-Klotz, N. *Prayers of the Cosmos: Meditations on the Aramaic Words of Jesus*. San Francisco: HarperSanFrancisco, 1990.

John of the Cross. *The Dark Night of the Soul*, in *The Collected Works*. Washington, D.C.: The Institute of Carmelite Studies, 1991.

Lewis, C.S. *A Grief Observed*. London and Boston: Faber and Faber, 1961.

Radin, P. *The Trickster: A Study in American Indian Mythology*. New York: Schocken Books, 1973.

God the Fox

Marti Matthews

I remember that day with reverence, awe, and a feeling of irony. I sat in silence on the porch of our beautiful old Yearly Meeting-house, facing the cornfields and the campgrounds in the walnut grove. It was early morning worship. Someone sat beside me; I believe it was Doris, a gentle elder of Illinois Yearly Meeting. Usually I would be inside, pulled into the Deep and Quiet and Holy with the dedicated and beloved Friends gathered for Yearly Meeting, but that morning I chose to join the renegades sitting in silence on the long porch.

As my eyes gazed absently across the road to the cornfield, I was startled to see the Fox. She seemed large for a fox, with a long beautiful tail; she was moving across the breakpath between the corn. She stopped in the path and sat looking directly at us on the porch. I nudged Doris' arm and she pinched my arm in return to say that she'd seen her also. For a moment we all sat still, Doris and I and the Fox; then she was gone, disappeared among the field of corn from which she'd come.

In the silence that remained I felt both joy and trepidation. I had come to know that to be visited by the Fox was an omen of change to come; God was on the move and about to ask change of direction from someone. The Unexpected could now be expected: God the Trickster had appeared in the form of the Trickster fox.

I cannot remember how I learned this. I believe my relationship with God the Fox emerged somewhere after the sudden death of my first Tom, my husband of twenty years. But that event had just seemed to bring to clearness how my whole life had been full of the Unexpected and that staying one with the Source of My Life has always required changing directions faster than is comfortable. I have always dragged my feet through life's changes, but kicking and screaming I've been led forward to many spiritual learnings that have surprised me. Perhaps only as Trickster could God have taught these to me; it may be my own stubbornness that has required God to open me up by turning my life upside down again and again. I have often felt tumbled and pushed to search for sense in confusion and find my way through fog, reaching out for help. I will share with you a few of the major tricks that life has played on me and what I was led to learn.

❂

As the first full day of Yearly Meeting moved on, soon I was presenting a committee report for Meeting for Business. I finished my report, but found myself spontaneously speaking then of the morning's visitation. 'The Fox has visited us!' I explained. 'This surely is a sign of something large being asked of us here at this session. Perhaps we will be asked to make some major change,' I suggested.

But the sessions moved on smoothly. There were no big conflicts, no major proposals; this was one of the smoothest Yearly Meeting gatherings we'd had in years. We came to the end without seeing why the Fox had appeared.

My second Tom and I had but a week to hurry home and prepare for our big trip to the southwest. We would represent Illinois Yearly Meeting at the 18th FWCC Triennial at Ghost Ranch, New Mexico. We had bought a little camper to make a trip out of it and we headed out joyfully across the prairies of southern Illinois, over the wide and lazy Mississippi and through the rolling green hills of Missouri, on through Oklahoma, Texas, and finally arriving at Albuquerque to visit a beloved Friend from Yearly Meeting.

New Mexico was awesome, like a different planet. Big skies and quietness like the open prairies of Illinois but different colors, and the land itself was both flat and mountainous, stark and warm. From Albuquerque we meandered northward toward Ghost Ranch, slowly rising higher into the gradually appearing mountains. As we turned down the dirt road to arrive at Ghost Ranch, Tom felt dizzy and asked me to drive the last few thousand feet. His dizziness passed as we signed up at the desk and found a campsite. The altitude was taking adjustment from his lungs, weak with emphysema. His dizziness came and went that evening and he slept well. At breakfast Sunday morning we sat socializing with Friends from Africa, England, Santa Fe, and other parts of the world. Suddenly Tom said, 'I can't move!' He sat frozen.

I had no idea what to do. The Friend from Santa Fe knew the grounds and jumped up to call on the phone for a nurse. Suddenly Tom fell over onto the floor. He needed oxygen. Someone suggested I bring my car around so we could get him to the infirmary. I ran for the car, but by the time I was back men were carrying him on a stretcher, running to the infirmary where hopefully there was oxygen.

At the infirmary there was no oxygen. An ambulance was called from the nearby town, but in the meantime Tom could neither speak nor move and his body was shaking uncontrollably. At the small local hospital, the kind staff could not tell what was happening and did not feel equipped to help him, so he was put again in an ambulance and we began the hour's drive to Santa Fe. By the time we reached Santa Fe the shaking had stopped but Tom was still unable to speak or move. An MRI scan showed finally that he had suffered a brain stem stroke, a blockage in the brainstem, which had completely paralyzed his entire body.

And so – this was it. The Fox had not appeared for the Yearly Meeting; the Fox had appeared to me. The happy path that Tom and I had walked together for only five years was suddenly stopped, and we were picked up and put down on a completely different path. For him it was the beginning of the end of his life; for me it was a testing of every resource I had within me. It would be another two and a half years now of the hardest work of my life and for Tom the most undesirable slow death any of us could imagine.

Tom was surely taken by surprise, yet he had known in some intuitive way that his end was coming and had tried to communicate it to me. His dying had begun three years before with the terrible accident of his only son at the age of twenty-eight. Mark had fallen seventy feet down a slanted wall while rockclimbing at Devils Lake, Wisconsin. I remember that night when Tom and Mark's mother were called to come to the next state, to the emergency room, and asked to decide their son's life or death, with no warning and no chaplain or social worker to guide. 'His brain is swelling,' the doctors had said. 'If we don't cut out some of his brain, he'll die.' They were unable to say what part they'd be cutting out, what the prospects might be, except that he'd die if they didn't do this. And so, the parents decided to give the boy a chance: part of his brain was cut out and he lived.

Now three years later it was evident that Mark was going to live for a long time in his strong young body but his brain could not function. He seemed to understand words – tears had come from his eyes when Tom told him we'd be going on this trip for three weeks! But he could give no output: he could not speak or move a muscle from his own volition.

Tom couldn't stand the pain of seeing his son in this condition. He'd written poem after poem expressing his agony and love for Mark. And a half-year before FWCC, Tom had written a poem in which he'd said goodbye to me, that something in him was now dead, he couldn't handle the pain of his life. I had read the poem but didn't have the foggiest how to react or what to do with it.

Looking back, this brings to memory the dreams and premonitions I had of my first Tom's heart attack – starting two years before he died. The Fox had given warning: there were intuitions and dreams, but I couldn't believe them, didn't know what to do with the information.

✪

The morning after (second) Tom's stroke I looked at him and said 'Tom! You've reduced yourself to the same state as Mark!' Both were now completely silenced and paralyzed. The father who could not save his son from his suffering had taken on his son's condition.

✪

Ninety percent of brainstem strokes die within three weeks, I was told. There is always the far, far chance of recovery, but it's more likely that he'll live in this paralysis for some time and then die anyway. Should we put a tracheotomy in his throat so his lungs can be kept clean? Should we put a G tube in his stomach to feed him? In other words, should we do these extraordinary things to keep him alive, the doctors asked me? I loved this man with whom I'd had this short but rich life, and I'd already lost my first Tom suddenly; how could I say, 'Let him die?' I was in turmoil. Finally I talked to a chaplain on the phone who asked if Tom was able to communicate. 'His mind is fine,' I reported. 'He communicates by closing his eyes for NO, raising his eyebrows for YES.' 'Then it's not your decision to make,' the chaplain clarified. I felt relieved, but so began the two and a half strange, horrible, and gifted years of slowly winding down Tom's life, slowly letting both of us get used to what had happened: the angel of death had appeared and there was no reversing this new course no matter what monumental effort we put against the odds.

I could tell you about these hardest years of my life, but they're a blur. Our many supportive Friends and friends could tell you better than I, as each present moment was so gigantic to me that there was no memory nor any sense of direction. I almost died myself of problems in my own body caused by caring for a man much bigger than myself that first year at home. I finally gave in, went with the inevitable direction and put him in a nursing home where I visited him every day, until that surprising moment when I walked in his room and saw that he'd fallen on his stomach, his face in the pillow, and he was finally finished with his long struggle. Death had been coming and coming and coming, yet when it arrived it was still a surprise, still the Unexpected, still the sense that in a moment my life was now again on some totally new path into an unknown future.

My will versus the Trickster's will

I think it's almost possible to say that my whole life has gone the opposite of the way I wanted it to go. The self-directed willful hero imaged for us by the moguls of worldly success is pure mythology to me; whatever I've wanted, the Unwanted is what has been asked or even demanded of me.

I never wanted to be a mother, but I was married back in my Catholic days; when we finally faced this issue my husband's loyalty to the Church caused confusion and in no time I found myself pregnant. I cried through the first four months of that pregnancy but began to adjust when the life within me started moving. By the time of childbirth I was amazed and felt gifted by this precious life that had become part of mine. I later had a second child to protect the first, as I still felt the pull toward other work so strongly and felt I needed to force myself to function as a mother. I love those two precious lives; perhaps they are my very best friends now as adults! Unexpected gifts on turns of path.

I have learned the danger of expectations. So often when I've tried to set a path, the Unexpected has jumped out in front of me and my task, my path, has changed. I've zigged and zagged through life, sometimes at a tremendous pace. There have been many things I've wanted to do and *have* done, within the context of these larger scenarios. But all in all, my own desires seem to have to follow some larger Desire. I am led where I would not go.

If I looked at my life through the eyes of the world I might feel justified in being cynical, faithless, sad, and bitter. Yet Grace has always felt present with me; I've made it through so many difficulties – somehow – and found myself enriched by all this weird experience I call 'my life'. It hasn't been as I would have chosen, but in all honesty I must admit it has been full of its own gifts. For this reason I come to the view that life is a dialogue with Destiny, and that we are guided through our lives wondrously by a Presence. I call that Presence the Fox, in jest I guess, and awe, at the unpredictable Power and Love that lead me on safely. Where are we going? And why must we go this way? In times of pause I ask these questions. But in these same times of pause I also ask, 'Where have we been?' and 'What did we learn there?' Then I see that where I was led was perhaps where I needed to be for my growth, more than where I would have chosen.

Dag Hammarskjöld, former Secretary-General of the United Nations, has expressed well what my experience has been:

> I don't know Who – or what – put the question; I don't know when it was put. I don't even remember answering. But at some moment I did answer *Yes* to Someone – or Something – and from that hour I was certain that existence is meaningful and that, therefore, my life in self-surrender had a goal.
>
> From that moment I have known what it means 'not to look back', and 'to take no thought for the morrow' (Hammarskjöld 1964: 201).

✸

It's certainly not the 'tragedy' aspect of the events of my life that makes me call Power by the name of 'the Fox'. I must let go of the judgment of words like 'tragedy'. One rule of the game – the instinct to survive – tells me that I cannot wallow in my emotions but must swim to the surface quickly, let the past go as swiftly as nature will allow, and just get on. I must re-orient myself to where I am now, try to figure out a new path from here, try to find the Guide and the Lighted Path. I cry hard when I'm crying, get it done with, and then get up off the carpet and go cook dinner.

I did that several times when my first Tom died at the age of forty-two, leaving me with our two teenagers to somehow get through college, me with a severe back curvature who'd stopped working two years before because it was hard to stand on my feet. That was certainly a night of destiny.

For several years I'd felt the call within me to write, but the upcoming challenge of paying for college caused my husband to encourage me to 'find a job, please?' I wrote when I could, and it always felt good. One September day I sat outside and wrote for the entire day; it felt so right that I finally gave in to the sense of calling and made the commitment to 'write as long as I'm able'. I climbed into bed at 11.00 p.m., and only then did Tom tell me that he'd been having pain in his left arm and shoulder all day. He hadn't wanted to interrupt me but told me now that he'd gone to an outpatient clinic where a doctor looked at his EKG and said she thought he was having a long slow heart attack. He'd gone then to the local hospital where the head of the cardiac unit said it wasn't a heart attack and sent him home with aspirin. We went to bed scared. He'd been to the hospital: what more could we do? Tom fell asleep saying, 'The most wonderful thing in all the world is to fall asleep in your arms.' At 1.00 a.m. I was awakened by a strange deep sigh. I jumped up, turned on the light, and realized that he was gone! Nothing the paramedics could do could bring him back; just like that he was gone.

Walking blindfolded on a lighted path
In that dark winter I did, in fact, several times lay down flat on the

carpet, unable to get up under the weight of the task before me. The only prayer I know in situations like this is one word: 'Help! I need help. Whatever Power there be in the world, please help me.' As the sages say, all things change, and to my amazement even this feeling of total helplessness would pass if I let it. I would eventually find myself standing again and somehow walking to the kitchen to do the next tiny step I could see to do. My chicks relied on me and I could not stay lying on the carpet. Somehow Grace lifted me and set me on the path again.

What path? How would I find my way through the brambles of the college tuition years? This I could not see, but each moment I found my footing for the next moment, and unexpected ways opened. This has been one of the challenges and great gifts of these impossible situations: when one cannot see the future one can only live in the present, and when life seems too much, one *must* open to the presence of Higher Power and guidance to survive. I have been taught to trust in Love without seeing ahead, and I have found that Love is there. My judgment about 'impossible' tasks has proved false. With Grace, I have done what seemed to me impossible, over and over.

The uncanny feeling of some strange rightness in my husband's death came from that coincidence about my calling to write. If it had been financially illogical to write before he died, it would be even more illogical after he died. And yet I'd felt clear to make that commitment, so as long as I was able that winter I did write. In January something strange came over (or through) me. For two months I found myself passionately writing my thoughts on pain and suffering, a subject I'd thought much about over the years because of my back curvature and the other various sufferings of my life. Then at some point I felt done; I'd said everything I had to say about why there's suffering in life and how to handle it. Then what? Another opening: High Tea with Madeleine L'Engle for those of us in Chicago who had taken courses from her. She had heard about Tom's death and I knew her own husband had died only a year before, so I took advantage of our commonality and brought my little manuscript under my arm for High Tea with Madeleine. She graciously took the manuscript home and read it, sent it back with real encouragement but told me I needed to tell more of my own story with these meditations.

My own story? I didn't want to talk about me, I wanted to share my hard-won insights on pain and suffering with others who were suffering. I puzzled for a few months until a Friend told me about the Patrick Henry Christian Writer's Scholarship at Earlham School of Religion (ESR). My son (Tom number three; actually, chronologically he's number two) was now at Earlham (bless them for their financial help to a needy Quaker boy). But how could I leave my daughter to go away and write? No sooner had I asked the question than the answer came. My son's girlfriend was planning to look for a job the very term that the scholarship was offered and she'd be glad to work in Chicago and be with Annemarie. So I applied for the scholarship – and won. At ESR, I went into a marvelous setting with friendly advice all around me from intelligent faculty and students, and my first book, *Pain: The Challenge and The Gift*, unfolded as if a carpet had been laid before it. The Fox does not always lead one through brambles; this was a surprisingly straight run. I followed the advice learned in Tom Mullen's class, 'Writing for the Religious Market', about how to find a publisher and lo! The first publisher I sent it to accepted it – after some negotiating, again using Tom Mullen's helpful ideas.

Would that the path of life always unfolded so smoothly, but of course these moments of ease seem occasional. What I experienced in that smooth unfolding had its own unique learning. Grace is with us. Sometimes the river flows easily, sometimes the river is rough and one must pay more immediate attention, but there's always a way unfolding and Guidance is with us. The hard times may actually be the better times because we then most know our limitations and feel open to the presence of the Love that Created Us.

Learning to live with paradox and mystery

Through my closeness to Death I've learned two contradictory truths. The first is that my life is a gift to me: I should use it thoughtfully, it may be taken from me at any unexpected moment as happened for my two Toms; my life is a gift to me and I'm responsible to care for it; I'm also free to be creative with it.

At the same time, my life is not my own. My life also belongs ultimately to Something that brought me into existence, with some intentions in mind it seems, and Something guides me through it – and that sometimes with a determined will.

Thirdly, the love of others that upheld my husbands and me through our hard times taught me that my life also belongs to the community. The community is not just kind when I'm suffering but the community helps because they need me! My gifts and those of my husbands are treasured and missed by others; in some sense they belong to others as much as to us. My life belongs to me and my life belongs to the community and my life belongs to the Source of All Life.

Living comfortably with Mystery, with unknowing, without judging what's happening (just evaluating where necessary) – these also are necessary changes I've come to make in order to follow the Fox. I love the way Winnie the Pooh describes this in *The Tao of Pooh*:

> When you work with *Wu Wei*, you have no real accidents. Things may get a little Odd at times, but they work out; you just let them (Hoff 1982: 78).
> [*Wu Wei* means effortless effort, swimming *with* the flow.]

That line – 'things may get a little Odd at times' – says a mouthful.

Traveling light

Another of the major challenges I've found in keeping up with the Fox is the need to travel light. The constant changing of direction at the speed that I'm led seems such a challenge; I realize that part of the difficulty lies in carrying too much baggage. I've not only accumulated material things but also such a large number of people I love, and then there are the wonderful experiences I want to savor in photos, or even better, to repeat.

With the slow death of my second Tom I had the awareness of all he had to slowly 'never see again': of possessions, of friends and family, of beautiful places and wonderful activities. Elisabeth Kubler Ross tells us that the final stage of dying requires this: that we stop caring about even the people we love the most, in order to make this last jump into the arms of the Source of Life. It seems to me that the swiftness of my leader, the Fox, requires this kind of death constantly. I have to hold onto things lightly. I cannot expect to see every friend again or to repeat every wonderful experience. I hold possessions as long as I'm truly using them and then try to get myself to pass them on with gratitude, trusting that what I need for the unknown future will be there, as the Fox seems in charge of this trip. I repeat experiences I've liked as opportunity offers. And I hold in my heart all those people I love. I 'hold them in the Light', as we Friends say, meaning for me that when I think of them I send my love and see them as thriving in their own lives. I ask the loving Source of Life to help them as they need. I keep in touch with friends as opportunity allows or as Spirit seems to call. Memory alone becomes my treasure chest. Only in this way can I keep up with the opportunities and challenges to which the relentless Fox continues to lead.

There is a growing list of unexpected things, which the cunning Fox asks me to relinquish in order to keep up as we travel. I've realized that even grudges are heavy and slow one down. I want to have a temper tantrum over this – that Life is so demanding I can't even afford to hold onto my petty grievances. I tend to be fond of my grievances as they seem to elevate my own value, but the Fox says 'No'; the Fox doesn't seem to care at all if others seem to devalue me. Maybe this is because there's a given between us – the Fox stays with me because the Fox values me, and the possible mistakes of others on this subject do not matter. And so I forgive – because it makes me lighter!

A similar burden I'm asked to lay aside is 'What will people think?' This fear has bound my feet for too long and must go. There just isn't time to worry about this when trying to stay in step with this swift Leader. When I can explain myself to others I try, as this is part of loving relationships and accountability keeps us honest. But 'following' (following the Fox), by definition, means that I must sometimes obey even when my own rational mind does not understand the Why.

I've had to practice at this, as not every impulse that comes to me may be a calling of the Fox. I try to allow the maximum time possible to 'sleep on' an illogical leading, to check it out in every way I can. But the Fox does not always allow me the luxury of pondering: I have had to learn to get clear quickly about whether Grace is or is not upholding a strange leading and to find the humility to obey.

Perhaps following on this is the demand to let go of undone projects. I feel sadness when I realize that I've dawdled in responding to an opportunity and now the Fox is moving again: I must abandon what might have been and keep up with the present moment. I may *never* finish or do what seemed an inspiration. The pain of regret wants to stay with me, but I can't even afford to carry this! Regret always has a little learning in it, and only the learning is what I'm allowed to take with me.

The confusion I feel by these undone projects has led me to the saving technique of using the word 'maybe.' I say 'maybe' to suggestions from others of wonderful things to do, and I say 'maybe' to myself when my creative mind sees something I 'could' do. I never know if the Fox will let me do any possible project. What I think is important and what the Fox thinks are often not the same. So, to any inspiration I say 'maybe' and then proceed to see if the Fox leads me towards or away from this.

At the same time, I've certainly had to learn to 'Never say Never;' this is definitely required of Fox followers. I never wanted to be a mother; even less did I ever want to do nursing. Currently I'm back in Michigan to be with my mother who's in a nursing home, depressed, and into the winding down of her life. I remember saying after my last Tom died that I wouldn't do this again (accompanying a loved one in their last difficult days), but after my recovery from Tom's death I find myself doing it again. What can I say? I just *never* know, I can only guess – where we're going next.

Fear is still a temptation and burden that wants to make me fall behind. Actually, fear seems to be the largest bundle that keeps me from running swiftly and from zigzagging with my fearless Leader. Because of fears I often put my brakes on, but eventually I find myself dragged forward anyway. The Fox knows no fear and calls to me to run freely. Here I remind myself of the well-phrased response of Rumi, the Sufi poet, in *Talking Through the Door*:

'Where can you live safely then?'
'In surrender.'

'Is there no threat of disaster?'
'Only what comes in your street,
inside your love.'
(Barks 1995: 78)

The Trickster teaches me the unexpected

In this fast-moving journey there have been demands that simply shocked me.

For example, many experiences of the last few years have seemed to want to teach me to let go of feeling responsible for others! In my upbringing, being sensitive to others' needs, being a caring helping person, was a must, and into adulthood I continue this leaning. But I've been learning that love does not always rescue. As I have a clear sense of being guided, I also feel more confident that everyone else is being guided, too, and are on their own strange paths that I may not understand. I've learned to help where I discern that I'm truly led to help, particularly where I'm *asked* to help, and not to jump in and try to rescue every person in difficulty.

Helping others without interfering in their opportunities to grow is very difficult. I want so much to take away the suffering of those

I love that sometimes I don't leave space for them to be responsible for themselves, to exercise their free will on their own behalf. Have I not learned that suffering is often a subjective word we give to the challenges of the inscrutable cunning Fox?

In getting to know my Leader I've come to realize how little the Fox values comfort! As a modern American, 'feeling comfortable' seems to me an essential part of the definition of peace and happiness. Yet the Fox does not seem to agree with me here: 'feeling comfortable' has no priority to This One in charge.

To accept the unacceptable: this is surely one of the hardest tests to which the Fox may lead us. The Unacceptable is the darkest of mysteries. I guess that I, too, had that test in staying with Tom through his slow silent dying. And now I find myself holding my mother's hand in her last days, to be with her as friend, unable to take away the pain and the inevitable end. I do this because I feel that love leads me to accompany her through her hardest challenge. Love often asks this of us, but I, too, then experience the suffering of 'watching'. It's one thing to face my own suffering, to grasp and find meaning in the brambles, but to believe the same for another who doesn't seem to be finding meaning in the brambles – this takes detachment, strong faith, and true love. I often think of Mary the mother of Jesus standing at the cross. There were those who loved him but could not do this. But the Fox calls some to this difficult task, and the calling is known because the strength is there to do it.

❁

Against these learnings about love, there is an opposite and surprising learning to which the Fox has recently led me: that I can overvalue people, and similarly overvalue myself. I seem to easily see the good in people and believe that each person is worthy of great investment of energy in support, nurture, etc. But in the past few years, experiences have pointed me again and again toward the strange idea that I've invested more in loving others than they deserved! Idealist that I am, and perhaps it's the 'mother' in me, I find it hard to devalue anyone, but this is what has been coming to me. What's helping me see this truth is the realization that I may also overvalue myself!

There is a paradox within a paradox here. It seems true that every individual is precious, unique, and worthy of great amounts of attention and energy. It is true that we were created out of love and the enthusiasm (breath) of the Source. At the same time, we modern humans as a species make too much of ourselves. Death, disasters, and all the Uncontrollable in life try to tell us our limits and offer us our proper place. Yet we are still stubbornly stuck in inordinate delight in our skills. It's good news that we do 'belong' here – we have an important place as individuals and as a species – but we belong in a larger scheme, we have a place alongside all the rest of creation and we are still 'subject' to power greater than ours.

For many years the frog has been a totem animal for me, but of late the ant also seems to be a guiding animal. I will explain this unexpected and humble guide. I recently spent time in Florida and shared a plot of ground with several large hills of red ants. My human neighbors considered ant neighbors to be a nuisance to get rid of, and that's easy to do, but I enjoyed their company. I felt amazed to watch the seriousness of these tiny lives, totally intent on their important enterprises. They seemed a mirror of us: all busy, busy, busy, doing things that seem so necessary, feeling our power as we efficiently go about grand endeavors. Yet to my eye, the ants were small, significant but also insignificant, and their sense of seriousness about themselves looked humorous.

While in Florida I also visited the Kennedy Space Center where I could see our world as it looks from outer space – so small in the Universe, precious to us but hardly the center of all that's going on. Shortly after this I flew home to Michigan ('flew'=by plane, of course) and had the delight of seeing the busy world of humans below me looking much as an anthill. We were even less than an anthill – one could never even see an individual person in their busy enterprises. I knew they were down there as one knows that amoebas exist after seeing them in a microscope, but my living busy human friends were as invisible as any microscopic life. This view combined with my ongoing experiences with the power of Death has helped bring me down to size.

Even our argument for our importance that humans supposedly have 'eternal souls', consciousness, and free will while the rest of the universe doesn't, seems more and more questionable to me, more a reflection of our own limits in perceiving what's going on in the rest of creation. We assume a lot about other animals, as we don't know their languages (we assume they should know ours) and we fail to perceive the intelligence that is holding other life forms in existence and what those forms are experiencing. The human delight in our own abilities is understandable, but the judgments we make on things we don't understand may be as humorous to the Fox as is the self-seriousness of ants. Perhaps the Fox seems a Trickster to us only because we are being led by quite a different point of view.

We have thought that we are made in God's image, but so also is all the rest of creation. We have limited God to our own image and refused to see how much larger is the Source of All That Is.

'Worship' seems to come hard for us these days. This happens as we make ourselves out to be more important and powerful than we are in the totality of the Universe. We *can* overvalue people. We can overvalue ourselves. Death is the ultimate truth-teller about the limited importance of our grand enterprises and powers. Death will take each of us when It wills, regardless of how important we feel our work to be. This reality should bring us back to 'following' and 'belonging', to living with things beyond our rational understanding, to 'worshipping' when it means bringing ourselves into alignment with the Love that owns us.

Worship is not an onerous task. Rather, it is freeing and energizing to bring ourselves back to remembering that we are not alone, and that we are not solely responsible for the course of events. Perhaps worship is no more than opening and accepting the Love that upholds us.

I recently saw a delightful Japanese movie called *Shall We Dance?* – the story of a responsible, weary Japanese businessman who is led against his rational mind to take up ballroom dancing. He's very awkward, of course, and his story involves many other people. One is a lovely young instructor who eventually tells how she danced in high competition and experienced a disaster: she and her partner bumped into someone and fell flat on the floor in front of the judges. She's never been able to deal with this crushing event. Among other confusing aspects of it, her partner – in gentlemanly fashion – should have fallen under her to protect her, but he didn't.

As she tries to teach this awkward businessman how to lead in dancing she also has to explain how the partner follows, and she has to try over and over to follow him correctly so he can learn to lead. It suddenly dawns on her what that great moment of failure on the competition floor was all about. She says, '*I was really dancing alone!*' She and her partner had been moving together on the floor for months, but she had never totally abandoned herself to his leading. 'I never totally trusted my partner,' she says, which is also why he couldn't protect her when they fell (Matthews 1987: 12).

To stand in the truth of our limitations, our createdness, is freeing. For over a year I've been awakening with a songline in my head. Morning songlines have been with me for years, the last part of my dreaming in which dreams seem to clarify themselves as though they were dealing with a very dense person, or at least a verbal person who doesn't grasp images well. This particular songline has been from the familiar Shaker song, 'The Gift to be Simple', and the emphasized punchline is this:

> 'Tis a gift to come down where we ought to be.
> And when we find ourselves in the place just right
> 'Twill be in the valley of love and delight.

I have actually resented this never-ending message from the deeps. Do I have myself so high up? But as I've realized that we *all* are in this place – overvaluing our place in the larger scheme of things, this has helped me come down, and it *is* a place of delight. When we come down to the right size we also come down to responsibilities we can handle. Often life feels like 'too much' because we're off the Lighted Path, we aren't 'following' and Grace is not upholding us in our self-assigned tasks. So the Fox has shown me what it means to overvalue both others and myself. I've learned to treasure us all while remembering our place in a system vaster and more yet unknown to us than we can begin to imagine.

Throwing the last weights overboard

Lastly, I'll tell you a surprising, similar, but not-exactly-the-same lightening to which the Fox has brought me. I call it a lightening because it's a shedding of limitations, and this allows me to stay more one with this Presence that's always wanting to take me into newness. First I learned that I/we can view our experiences from too 'personal' a point of view. Some humans seem to be too impersonal, but perhaps because of my experience in motherhood I'm of that other leaning: my whole world seems centered around the personal. I've felt surprised to realize the limitations of the personal. But I've experienced the freedom of non-attachment to myself as 'Marti,' that I can experience myself separate from the body and personality that I usually call 'me'.

I was helped in this discovery by an old rather silly movie called *Cocoon*, a movie about senior citizens in Florida encountering aliens from another planet who gave them the possible power not to age. These friendly aliens were actually 'light beings' wearing human costumes; they could unzip their costumes at will and function as pure light. This is what I've discovered is possible! The identity I wear as 'Marti' is pretty tight, like a diver's wetsuit, but one can unzip a wetsuit and get out of it, and in periods of stillness one can shed the over-identifying we do with all our personality and bodily characteristics. One can find the way back to one's self before one was born! We, too, are light-spirits; this is not a metaphor but one can actually experience this.

✦

Is there anything left? Keeping up with the Fox requires more flexibility of thinking and more letting go than I could have ever imagined. Perhaps I'm a turtle trying to keep up with a fox. Yet the Fox seems persistent and sly in dealing with me, and it does seem that the unpredictable, swift-moving, and sometimes-seemingly-heartless Fox will demand it all. The Fox and I will zig and zag and hurry forward till suddenly – still Unexpectedly – I'll find us at the end, the goal for which I was born. Yes, there is still that total detachment to do. What trick will the Trickster have to come up with to persuade me to do this? I suspect my attachment to life will still have me clinging and it will take a major and creative persuasion to get me to let go. I'm sure the Trickster will come up with something. Perhaps if I keep trying to swim with the flow instead of against it, if I put my effort into trusting and following, I will at that last point be light and swift enough to be one with my leader, the Fox, Who has led me safely home.

> Thou
> Whom I do not know
> But whose I am.
> Thou
> Whom I do not comprehend
> But Who hast dedicated me
> To my fate.
> Thou.
>   (Hammarskjöld 1964: 214)

References

Barks, C. *The Essential Rumi*. San Francisco: HarperCollins Publishers, 1995.

Hammarskjöld, D. *Markings*. New York: Alfred A. Knopf, 1964.

Hoff, B. *The Tao of Pooh*. New York: Viking Penguin, 1982.

Matthews, M. 'As If We Are Perfectly Safe: On Fear, Faith, and Destiny'. Jonathan Plummer Lecture, Illinois Yearly Meeting, 1997.

Tricks and Angels

Ben Pink Dandelion

Part of me lies by the side of a road in Germany. I crashed my motorcycle there in September 1997 and whilst I can now walk and work again, I feel part of me got left behind.

I walk the paths and ride the roads now as a different person, one who is learning to let go. Letting go of all I was brought up to be, all the counter-visions I made for myself. Learning to let go of my self. To realise 'I' am not what matters. And yet the journey described here is all about a 'me' I watch and observe and judge, and one I feel is judged by God. Paradox. Self and not-self. Quietist Friends struggled with this all the time in their attempts to 'annihilate self' along the 'wearisome pilgrimage' of life. I struggle with this tension now, vainly holding onto all my self-definitions and self-importances whilst knowing that at one level I am not even worthy to be a crumb under the table.

I believe I have been resistant to God's leadings in my life and that tricks have been a crucial part of 'waking me up' to a truth beyond my own making. This article looks in particular at the lessons I have needed to learn about life with God using what has been most important in my own self-definition in order to get towards a more Divinely-defined life.

An unaccompanied life

The accident was a reminder from God that I have been called to live a life unaccompanied, except by God.

Since the age of nineteen, I have been involved in hundreds of sexual relationships. The first compulsion was to try and erase schoolboy taunts about my body, about my physical potential and abilities. I have carried layers of shame about my body since those days and to be 'wanted' sexually was a way to try and ignore that. The second compulsion, related, was to feel uniquely necessary in some kind of way. Only in the throes of passion with another have I ever felt, albeit so temporarily, indispensable. For some reason, it has been important for me to feel useful, and this has been the arena I have found that sense of utility most readily.

I have not been monogamous, other than for a brief spell. Ideology, then temperament, took me away from that path. I have also come to see that I am frightened of intimacy, a fear underpinned by the physical shame, an inability to be exclusive in my affections, and a desperate determination for freedom. I have not prioritised intimacy as society does.

My sexual relationships usually end quickly. I have ended up with a list of standard reasons as to why the sexual part of my relationships ends sooner rather than later. For example, the other would want monogamy, or children, or more time, or less religion, or a hunkier lover, or one of a different sex, and also to be with someone who saw the sexual life as the icing on the cake of the relationship, not as marginal or optional.

In 1995, I met the woman I may have loved the most. We felt our relationship, whilst not an obvious one for either of us, was one led by God. When she ended our relationship, I called her a blasphemer. However, we both learnt through that time of calling. She claimed she learnt to be obedient to God even in the crazy. The relationship with me was a mad idea, the last thing imaginable to her, but she learnt to say 'Yes' to God, so that when her true love came along, another crazy calling on the face of it, she was ready to leave me to take hold of the new God-given opportunity. She had learnt her lesson of obedience to God through our relationship. For me, I came to be that close to her so that I would hear God's calling in my life from someone I wouldn't discount. When she told me later, 'I could not have chosen you ... you cannot be chosen' , I took it as a message from God.

I saw then that the way in which my parents had been taken away from me by early death, and the lack of any other direct family, was also perhaps part of the picture of one who had been called to live an unaccompanied life. The years of sorrow over being alone, of being sad that no one needed to know where I was, were replaced by a huge burst of energy at the ownership of freedom and clarity.

I have kept in touch with all my significant loves and they are amongst my best and dearest friends. This, and my marginalisation of the sexual (I wanted sex but not for it to carry emotional weight within the relationship), the desire to see it as optional, led me to realise that I really wanted friendship, not relationship. I came to see that I was really to have simply friendships, which may or may not be sexual. Not relationships. Not to use the language of relationship when I wasn't interested or capable.

I carried on my sexual life in this new way. After all, sex was wonderful. God-given and often God-present. Humanity remained beautiful. Sex was a natural and loving way to express desire and care. The hurt of all those endings was outweighed by the joy of beginnings. So I continued a sexual life, but within this new frame of friendship and without entertaining settled human accompaniment. I was even clearer with prospective partners that our relationship could go nowhere, for there was nowhere for it/me to go. Indeed, there was no 'it' to go anywhere. We were just friends. People continued to get hurt by misreading my gushy romanticism but less than before. I encouraged others to find someone else, knew I could only ever be a bonus, additional to their happiness elsewhere, that the sexual aspect of our friendship would be temporary. That, even for those dearest to me, I would 'knock at the back door of their lives' and that sometimes, they would be so busy or happy out the front that they would not hear me or need to. At other times, I would be welcomed in. The main thing though was that I would continue to knock because I was free to do so. I had no front-room life other than with God.

In particular, I became close with those who lived a long way away. They didn't expect to see me too often and actually saw a lot of me given the distance. I could be a good friend to someone 6000 miles away, a lousy one to someone round the corner. I would want to see them about the same amount, in spite of common assumptions that friends see a lot of each other. I would tell those more local, 'geography is accident ... pretend I live in Istanbul, unless you live in Istanbul – then pretend I live in London.' I just happen to be here not seeing you. I could be somewhere else not seeing you. As I've said, one of the reasons people left was wanting more of my time.

In February 1997, a rather awkward thing happened. I opened the door to a visitor I had never met before and instantly fell in love in that Hollywood kind of a way. I could hardly leave for my other engagements that evening, wondered if I was crossing God not to stay, and found time the next morning to stay a little longer in this woman's company. Later that year, I would see her again in her own country and in a mutual rush of romantic everythings, I rode away from her on my motorcycle believing I was heading in the wrong direction. I was also full of the thought that I could actually create a future out of all this I was feeling.

For the next weeks as I toured continental Europe by motorcycle, I held her close in my thoughts and my dreams, and hatched all kinds of plans to live closer to her. Then the motorcycle accident. And in the recuperation time, a chance to travel and to see her again, and to find out that the situation was not as mutual as I had dreamed, and that, also, she had totally fallen for someone else. I have only totally fallen in love six times but that is often enough to now be able to write the 'I'm sorry but ...' script. I crumbled, I wept, I rejoiced (for her, and maybe a little for me out of my place of fear), and still I loved this person, and in amidst all my own pain and confusion, sincerely wished the new relationship well. All those acknowledged elements of facing loss (denial, anger, bargaining, depression, acceptance) collided simultaneously as they do in these situations.

But for the motorcycle accident, I might have returned to England in ignorance, and without having been reminded of my calling not to be chosen. Unable to move in a German hospital bed, totally dependent on people I could not even understand, liberated from all responsibility, I could begin to see that there was a deeper second meaning to this, as there is to everything. Who was I to begin to imagine that I might live a settled life with another human? Who was I ... ?

As with the prior love, I believe God had used what was most dear to me to find a way for me to listen. My motorcycle, my major passion, was dead. My dreams were dead. Both were to be buried on that road in Germany. I had been called back into line.

Nothing was broken, except pride. I had had a motorcycle accident just big enough to achieve what was required. God gave me what I needed to be reminded about what I was being called to, though it was a beginning of a longer lesson too.

Some other part of me was left behind. By 'accident', my hair was shaved off in Berlin as I recuperated, but I knew it was a symbol of penance (Job 1: 20). That I hadn't just wronged God *this* time but in all my hedonistic pursuits which had led to such hurt over 15 years of sexual life. By January 1998, I had decided against beginning any sexual relations with those with whom there was an obvious incompatibility, e.g. monogamous, those wanting children, time, etc. In the past I had just denied these incompatibilities, colluding with the other that it would all be alright, that the other might change ...

By February 1998, I had come to see my greed more fully as an addictive pattern and resolved not to initiate *any* new relationships. I began to try to make amends for my past patterns, wrote several letters of apology. I saw just how far my denial had turned into the misleading of others, a lack of transparency on my part, even manipulation of their Noes into Yeses. I had behaved shamefully. I had used ideology and my full diary to defend my lifestyle and my life.

The façade had cracked and I came face to face with the fear that lay beneath it. I wrote around that time:

> and sex, and even making love, and the path to freedom, now only brings me more and more face to face with a world that is getting smaller. People linked with people, people linked with the past, and all the growing fears moving in decreasing circles above me, like vultures awaiting the dead. This global and ever-widening attempt at total freedom, so ironically and delicately tied to a desperate fear of losing anyone, can only end with the necessity to confront all I am running away from ... as the world closes in, and the life I was brought up to lead nudges at me relentlessly and seductively, but with only death of those dreams a Divine possibility in my life.

By May 1998, I found it impossible to be sexual with anybody at all without grave distress. Orgasms had always been like a death, good ones taking me to heaven, orgasms in situations which were inappropriate taking me down. I felt crucified, a tin opener skewering me down the front, exposing me to myself. It was a similar experience to the accounts I read of early Friends turning to the Light. Through the armour my fears of intimacy threw up, the tin opener of this painful ecstasy went for the guts. Sex was no longer an easy way out, ideology-defended passion. I was faced only with intimacy in sexual encounters and could no longer cope. Maybe I could have been sexual with the six I'd totally fallen for but all were with others, all abroad. I didn't mind not being able to find out. Instead I ran for cover:

> and yes, I am frightened of intimacy, but also know it needs to be limited, if only to avoid extreme discomfort, given the impossibility of following that path in any one direction.

I renegotiated, to my acute embarrassment, my sexual relationships into non-sexual ones, and became an emotional and tactile recluse. When a break in work afforded it, I became a geographical one too. I felt inadequate, impotent, unable to function fully, as if I were back in the hospital unable to walk. I existed, not lived.

Outwardly, my life was successful. Inwardly, it became a hollow shell. All that had given meaning to a meaningless life, i.e. my sexual addiction, had gone, and I was left with a vacuum, no criteria by which to spend time, decide what might be right. My thread of logic and meaning had snapped. I came to realise that all the sex had done nothing to relieve my sense of physical shame, of personal futility. Now though, I had the awareness of that condition, saw that any attempts to cover it up were delusion, and had Faith to carry me through the less compelling parts of this reality.

A friend once said of his call to marriage that it was as if God had said, 'well, until you can do this for me, you cannot be of use to me'. I felt a similar forest clearing. That the whole complexity of my sexuality, my driving force for personal freedom and self-esteem, for meaning in life, had been taken away now that perhaps it was no longer necessary.

Hiccups of sexual desire were only temptations to remind me of my distress. A friend of mine had once said she was frightened of breaking into a thousand pieces if she had an orgasm: I now lived this experience with each sexual encounter. God had always been part of the sexual for me. Now God brought a sledgehammer to bed, as well as the tin opener. There seemed no valid sexual life (it would either be empty lust, misled friendship or impossible and multiple love) and the paranoias crashed in, amplified through other insecurities. People required and deserved better lovers, better companions.

From being so actively bisexual, the men I thought most about now were the partners of those six I had totally fallen for. These were the men around whom I now needed to negotiate time. And yet, when I looked at those paired lives I came into occasionally, I knew I could not change places with any of the partners. That was much too scary and inappropriate for someone with my gifts. I could only be additional. This was the reasonable price of freedom, the consequence of my calling.

I gave up the sexual lens through which I had viewed the world. I was embarrassed, felt inadequate but at least 'faithful'. Then, fourteen months after the motorcycle accident, the woman I had been dreaming of that summer suddenly rang me from Heathrow airport and came to see me. It was the first time we had met since that summer. We had four hours together before this beautiful woman wandered off up the road to another country. A hug at the beginning, a hug at the end. I didn't want to let go of her, but I did and I will. I will remain as detached as she needs me to be, as is comfortable and appropriate. I give thanks for the love she has found in her life, so evident as she talked about her partner (and of course am in some way relieved that she has found what she needs elsewhere). And whilst I knew she would have to leave, I also thank God that she bothered to come and visit in the first place. That was a gift.

Once, we had seen our lives, separated by nation, in terms of a temporary 'now' and a future 'always'. Later, she had told me, 'But Ben, there can never be an always …' I trust there will be an 'always' of sorts. An 'always' in its own way. We are out of the Hollywood movie that marked our first meeting, into one of those French films that seems to end at an arbitrary moment mid-life. The movie carries on, but the viewers have to go home. I have so many movies running in my head. I live them all, constantly in front of the camera, hoping to hear the Holy Director's 'Cut!' This four hour visit was like an angel coming by. Reaffirming what I knew. A channel for the love of God amidst any inappropriate disappointment. Critically, I asked myself in the aftermath of that visit, my soul still so filled with hers, how I could be sexual with anyone for whom I didn't carry such a depth of feeling? I realised that I had arrived at a linear consequence of seeking my freedom above all else. That solitude, if painful at times, is lined with the joy, for me, of independence. That the absence of family gave me freedom from commitments. That I had been chosen, particularly once temporarily, to be shown that I was not to be chosen. That I had fallen in love in even the most dramatic fashion to hear that this was not to be part of my 'always'. As I sat on the outside of my life, looking in, as I look in on the lives of those six, I came to see so clearly how these angels were sent to educate me.

Daily life

I adopted a Rule in 1998. It included, amongst other things, a commitment to regular prayer and corporate worship, to continuing to shave my head as penance until I was more at ease with my present and my past, not to initiate new relationships and not to take on new pieces of work without testing them in group discernment.

As an anarchist, I had remained unemployed for eight years. I had since had three Quaker jobs and was working as Quaker Studies Tutor at Woodbrooke at the time of the motorcycle crash.

Going to work at Woodbrooke was a very real problem for me. I wasn't going to apply for the job, except that I was persuaded to join a group of people who were applying as a kind of 'dream ticket'. One of those people wasn't interviewed. One of those people was interviewed and not given the job, and I was given the job with two people, one of whom I'd never met before. I think I'd been clear it wasn't that all of us were to be given a job or none of us would accept. But even during the interview I was thinking 'No. I'm not the right person. Definitely not the right person. I can't teach. I'm clear about that.' Hoping, all the way down the line that other people would take the decision, that Woodbrooke would ring up and say, 'Well Ben, thanks for coming along to the interview, putting on a tie but, er, sorry.' But they rang up and said, 'Well Ben, we'd like to offer you the job.' All the way down the line I didn't say 'No,' hoping all the time other people would say 'No'.

At first, regularly, my classes went terribly, in my opinion. At least once a term. When it happened, I was so embarrassed that I couldn't look people in the eye afterwards. I just retreated to my room. On one occasion, I wrote to a Quaker friend, 'My soul is torn by the failure of a class today. And yet there is something about being in that wide open and vulnerable space which is so important. There is a lesson in the failure.' But my emphasis was very much on having failed. That I had fallen short, sinned. A student had asked me a question about what sin is, and after they went to that class I dropped them a note saying 'Now you know what sin is'. It is to fall short. It is to be separated from God. And I ended this note, 'Yours in the void between heaven and earth'. That sense of being accompanied, of living in a foretaste of the Kingdom had been skewed. So I was torn open. Torn open as I am regularly in the silence. Regularly as I am in close intimacy with others, placed on the cross, feeling the heaven and the earth inside me in contest, or not feeling them there at all but seeing how they are reflected in all that is between, in a kind of purgatory.

I got a reply from my friend which put me in my place. 'Sweet Brother I am in prayer that this day is indeed restful for thee. The failure in the class may be just where it needs to be for God's transforming love to be felt.' And then, most significantly:

> If thee was taking this failure in the class as thy failure, wast thee also counting the success of a class as thine, rather than God's through thee? I ask that in deep love and in the knowledge that thee does give the glory to God hoping that the sharp contrast will remind thee that we are not in control and so must constantly be seeking God's presence and gifts in all situations.

It is a very simple but clear reminder, speaking totally to my condition. I'm not in control. It's not up to me to decide 'Who am I?' If it had been a 'spanner in the works' to take the job at Woodbrooke, the spanner was God's. God the Trickster had given me a job which helped me learn so much.

Over time, the job felt easier. It still meant living away from my home in London for most of the time, but I began to feel part of the organisation and enjoyed the tremendous riches of colleagueship and of the students I met. Then, in the same summer as my sexual revolution was taking place, Woodbrooke announced it was to be reorganised for the future. The kind of teaching I most enjoyed and learnt from was to go; term-time to be replaced by short-courses.

I was alone in the world because I had designed it that way and passionately wanted it that way, and I had God sitting on my shoulder, watching, waiting, holding out a finger to steady me at these more fragile moments. Alongside the realignment of my inward and private life, I realised the outward shell, the outward success would have to go too. I was wary and cynical of *all* I had constructed to defend myself against the reality of societal meaninglessness. No life was wholly legitimate for me. As Woody Allen's character in his film *Deconstructing Harry* said, 'I came to realise we are all given the same truth – we just distort it in different ways.'

For someone concerned about his greed and power, it felt right to start declining invitations to speak, and part of my Rule was to withdraw from a public Quaker life. Someone had replied to a letter from me saying they had been flattered to get it, and I was so sad to be perceived in this way. I realised that alongside dismantling my version of my inward self, I had to dismantle the outward me. I had to dismantle this power. Especially as a man.

I knew it was time for me to lay down the work I had been doing. Again, a huge release of energy at feeling I was discerning correctly. It was also exciting to contemplate a life more at home, albeit on a much reduced income. It all fitted. The timing was perfect. As it was, my expenses had diminished with the end of continually chasing after new romances. I had fewer vehicles to maintain after the motorcycle crash. I was being led into a wholly new life.

Boys' stuff

God was working on all areas of my life. With a personal life too unorthodox or private for colleagues to ask about, I have always been well known at work for my passion for classic cars and motorcycles. When I killed the motorcycle in Germany, I sold two cars and two bikes to buy a replacement motorcycle. I had 24 hours of vehicular purity (i.e. owned none!) but then succumbed to a lovely red Moto Guzzi. An old bike, far less refined than my erstwhile BMW sports-tourer. Symbolic of a new kind of motorcycling life.

I wonder if it will have to go too, one day. Is the bike just another constructed identity which gets in the way of God? (God the Trickster working with exactly what I prize the most to give me what I need?)

The deliberate planned reduction of income and expenditure put me into a quandary. I had a weekend in the Lake District with a family who had almost been my own as a teenager. When I ended up walking the dog down the country lanes one morning, it was far too reminiscent of my lost childhood, lost sense of family, to be comfortable. When I later got to drive their 1927 Lancia, I was completely unsettled. I chose the easy route through the distress and dived into the motoring world once again, sure I was to buy a 1930s car. There followed a time of car auctions, weekly car newspapers, car magazines.

I know this behaviour. I knew it was covering up my occasional grief at being without family. Cars, for me, are about sharing, and the vision was to share this resource. It was a companionship-led vision. Was I also seeking power? Or a sense of utility to replace the sexual in my friendships?

I could not really afford such a car, and it would have taken me out of the simple-life movie into the 'eccentric academic with some money' movie. It would tie me to more work. I came to realise, that this rush of enthusiasm was the dying embers of a life that was not to be. A recycled holy testing process which was easier to get right.

This may be boys' stuff. Not just because it is about cars. It is about men coming to realise they will not be all that they have been brought up to be. I remember being in a men's group when I was 20. All the other group members were in their thirties. It was the year Boris Becker won Wimbledon aged 17. These men were so undone by this. They knew then they would not now win Wimbledon, a symbolic goal equivalent to whatever their own teenage dreams had been. I have heard it described as a 'crisis of limitation'. I was brought up to succeed in my father's footsteps. My father had been seen as even more perfect after he had died so unexpectedly and so tragically early and it was almost as if I was to be God's son; to go to Oxbridge, to be whatever I chose to. I ended up working for a religious group, such a sad and distressing outcome from the viewpoint of my atheist upbringing. I never gained the wealth or the lifestyle expected of me. At 17, I had cycled half way across the world. In my twenties I had worked for the revolution. At 35, plateaued, I realised I had been deluding myself sexually and in all manner of other ways. I was an ex-anarchist who had become a home-owner with a respectable job. Only my name safeguarded total assimilation into the world I had once rejected so vehemently. After years of being a vegan, I was even eating meat again. This was not the *Boys Own*-story fame and adventure I had always imagined for myself.

To lose sleep over a car just seemed pathetic, from either viewpoint. Either pitifully sad from the point of view of the anti-car purist or incomprehensibly sad from the perspective of the car fanatic.

I cannot explain this 'thing' about cars and bikes. It isn't just a car. It is a deep passion, 'something in the blood'. Maybe a calling. A 'ministry of transport' I would have joked in former times, certainly one of my chief sources of joy and interest. Movies and wheels. But at this time, not to own. And so it is too with the teenage dreams. They are not mine to have and I have to move into another movie still, one of acceptance. Not a romantic place. Not a place of fame. I have been given them to reject them. *Even* them.

I need to dismantle my power, to interrupt the management of self I am so accomplished at. To stop living in the eye of others. Dreams can be tricks too, or a part of Divine trickery.

So ... ?

We don't always know the reasons for God's work in our lives. Sometimes, we can retrospectively rationalise the past in terms of finding God's will in what has gone before. At other times, we are left not knowing. Or not knowing for a long time. We just know the change, feel the difference, sense its source.

So it is with me now. As work patterns change, as a whole new life opens up before me, I sit and wait for what further new light will be emptied into my open and hollower husk. I have to sort out all the intimacies I began before the revolutions of early 1998 but know that they will find their place in my life.

I know and always have known that life is meaningless, that all is constructed on this plane. I feel bitter and cynical at my own constructions, my own distractions. The way I rush to the small-ads when feeling bad. The way I only meet with people when I am feeling okay. My Quakerism. My critique of Quakerism.

Nothing is legitimate. God has called me on that one.

Reminded me.

Played with *exactly all* that I was playing with most passionately.

I love that Holy style, the continual learning, the perpetual not-knowing. It is an incredibly exciting time.

Walking Between the Worlds: The Divine Mystery and Trickery of Moab

Michele Lise Tarter

It must have been that last detail which drove me aimlessly to the desert of Moab: the doctors had decided it was best to put a feeding tube into my dying stepfather's stomach. Something about this detail pushed me beyond all boundaries, after years of living in the midst of his terminal illness. 'Why would they burrow a hole into this man's belly,' I asked myself, 'when every cell and fiber in him is suffering and longing to be released from his agony?'

Anyone who has lost a friend or relative to cancer knows all too well the anguish of watching the loved one suffer, deteriorate and wrestle with this all-consuming disease. For two years, my family and I witnessed Haeb slowly debilitate from a 300-pound 'Falstaff'-of-a-man to a very thin, aged, and frail shell. The cutting irony of this battle was that his voice, which had saved hundreds of lives throughout his profession and life-service as an attorney, was the very source of his malignant tumor: throat cancer. The second and more cutting irony was that this man – who enjoyed eating and drinking more than any human being I'd ever known – was now forced to sacrifice in large measure the very experiences he had so dearly treasured. With each phase of medical treatments, his throat continued to swell outwardly and tighten inwardly, until he could only sip liquids with short swallows.

Although it was my last year of the Masters Degree at the University of Colorado, I flew home seven different times, longing to be present with him and supportive of my family through this crisis. We wheeled his body in and out of chemotherapy treatments, radiation applications, and visits to the speech therapists who trained Haeb to speak, albeit briefly, with a voicebox device. There were hundreds of appointments, a band of doctors, and a house filled with medical equipment to help us counteract this disease, but in the end I realized that it had become all of us: it was ubiquitous, overtaking our thoughts, our spirits, our very identity, as we walked beside Haeb every step of the way.

When he asked – on his chalkboard – if he could go to Cancun for a last visit to the sea, we sent him with our blessings. He had gone through tremendous struggle so graciously and courageously; the chemo and radiation treatments were finished, but only to grant him a few more months of life. He went alone to the island, waded in the ocean each day, read on the sand, slept in the balmy air; and then he came home, ready to die. But in the hospital, the doctors insisted on prolonging his life as much as possible, and found their decision of a feeding tube to be the solution.

Back in Colorado and attempting to study for my Masters exam, I knew – logically – that I should be by Haeb's side in that hospital to care for him and my family. He and I had formed a very close bond through nonverbal communication over the past two years, and I could read his thoughts quite easily and assist him in so many ways because of this. Often, his eyes would just turn to me, and God gave me the vision and clarity to read them at once. Wasn't this reason enough to get home immediately? But try as I might to hurry back to Philadelphia, something kept stopping me, body and soul. My mind was cluttered with so much noise: images of hospitals, city traffic, Haeb's chest marked with radiation x's in blue dye; people crying in the waiting rooms, doctors' offices, cans of Ensure. Then it would shift to my Masters exam: details of Jane Austen's eighteenth-century world; Huckleberry Finn floating down the Mississippi; Chaucer's Troilus and Cressida trying to fall in love, against all obstacles. The clutter just kept magnifying, and then it snapped.

It came rather abruptly, when it came: I woke up one Thursday morning, withdrew from the Masters exam list, and called my mother to say I was heading west for a while; when she asked me why, all I could answer was, 'I'll tell you when I get back.' I then got in my car with my nextdoor neighbor Rosemarie, and, with camping gear in the trunk, we headed to Moab, named after the excluded con-gregation of the Lord (Deut. 23: 3). It was this land, and only this land, which was calling me with piercing sound. 'But how could I take off at such a critical moment?' I repeatedly asked myself on this long drive across the mountains. 'What was pushing me forward, when all logic and training told me I should go home and help my beloved family?' It just wasn't like me, and I began to fear that God would desert me, in turn, for such a self-indulgent, potentially careless and irresponsible act. Yet, my body plowed forward, even when my thoughts kept looking backward to the hospital bed in Philadelphia.

The orange slickrock of Moab is an extraordinary shrine to the newcomer. It burns bright against the azure blue sky and sizzles where the Colorado River winds through the valley. The rocks form many mystical images, such as the Three Sisters who welcomed us to this retreat. Rosie and I pitched our tent and settled into the sand, hungry to soak in this vast field of salmon skin, this ancient rock of vision and voice.

By nightfall, we craved the company of locals, longing to hear stories other than our own. To the Main Street bar we ventured, seating ourselves at a large, round table. It was only moments until a group of river raft guides saw us and moved over to introduce them-selves. Yet, I suddenly felt estranged, a foreigner to everything and everyone around me. While Rosie engaged more and more in jovial conversation, I retreated step by step, inching my way to the periphery. Nearly tucked in a dark corner of the room, I realized it was a mistake to have come here in my state of mind, and my heart longed to be nestled in our tent with my body resting upon the earth.

He came out of nowhere, so it seemed – a gentle but sound figure, nearly an illusion in this bar on Main Street. A Ute Indian in Gap jeans, he walked in and ordered something to quench his thirst, but while he waited, he turned and looked directly at me in the corner with his eyes of compassion; then he walked over to me without pause. Our gazes were locked a long time before anyone spoke: how well I knew this form of communication, because of Haeb. Slowly, then, he said: 'There is a place I want to take you tomorrow. Will you come with me?' Normally, every red flag of my instinctual body would be set off by such an invitation from a strange man, but I continued to look at him and to rest in this feeling of connection, especially at a time when I was feeling so drained and empty and alone on the parched cancer trail. I found myself answering 'Yes', softly, not quite believing he'd ever find our tent in the middle of the desert. He left as quickly as he came, never receiving any directions to our campsite, and I was certain he and I would never meet again. But when he appeared the next morning, my belly quivered and I knew he had been sent by the spirits of this holy land.

With Rosemarie by my side, we first drove with him in my car for many dusty miles, winding farther and farther off the beaten track and closer to the canyon walls. Then when the road ended, we stepped out and left behind the twentieth century, breathing in the ancient winds of Moab's Canyonlands. With no speaking at all, this man led us down a nearly invisible path, meandering through sage brush as he, with large and determined eyes, clearly sought some marker in the stones. It seemed only seconds before he stopped walking and pronounced, 'We are here.'

He turned to us, and then to the huge stone standing before us. My eyes followed his, and I beheld a massive rock which had been placed in this position as a sort of gateway; on it stood a looming pictograph, chiselled by Ute elders' hands, of a figure with his arms raised up, beckoning caution. 'This path was reserved only for the healers of my people,' he shared; 'Others were forbidden to walk this road. But you are invited to enter with me now.' Those were the final words for this journey. We entered through a blessed channel – a narrow passageway carved between trees and rock, as if we were being born to something both old and new in the crossing.

Once the rhythm of this hike became meditative, my thoughts moved instantly toward Haeb. Again with tinges of panic, I felt guilty for deserting him, for not being there by his side as he struggled near death. And I questioned why I was in the middle of nowhere, following this stranger deeper and deeper into a canyon. Then the sun took hold of my thoughts, as we left the shelter of the trees and were instantly vulnerable to its hot pulse and pressure on our flesh. Dryer and dryer it made us – as dry as the dust beneath our feet. I kept trying to swallow but couldn't. I was dying for a drink of water and utterly tempted to ask this man for a sip from the bottle he carried. Yet, I somehow didn't want to break the silence we three carried, walking among the ancestors in this temple of rock.

And, more poignantly, I suddenly realized that Haeb felt this parched and thirsty every day of his life. I found myself embracing this suffering, connecting to him more viscerally with every step, every breath. My very last interaction with Haeb came vividly to mind: pulling my face to his, his lips formed words without sound – 'I want to drink a gallon of lemonade.' And then, as now, I couldn't fulfill his wish, and it tormented me. That unquenched desire, that frustration, that insatiable thirst led me deeper into this channel, hot and parched with a will larger and stronger than I. Feeling as if I had been led between the worlds, I prayed to Haeb with every cell in my being: 'I am with you, Haeb, on each step of this journey. See what I see; leave your hospital bed for a few hours. Behold this orange rock, these timeless winds, this divine passageway.' And I knew at that moment that we had connected more strikingly than ever before.

Turning a corner ahead, Rosie lost all control as she heard the sound of running water, so desperately wanting relief from the oppressive and ubiquitous sun. While she ran to look for its source, I was certain it must have been a mirage – and yet, as if it were the continuation of this seeming dream, we soon discovered a waterfall cascading over boulders and collecting in a large, cool swimming hole. Within seconds, Rosie had thrown off her clothes and jumped into that water with ecstasy, calling back to me, 'Miiiche, jump in with me and I'll be your best friend!' I watched her splash around with water drops glistening on her face and hair, but I just couldn't move. I'd gone deep into this connection with Haeb, and I didn't want to shift out of it.

I sat down and soaked in Rosie's delight, all the while remaining devoted to what Haeb was feeling and undergoing, moment by moment. It was then that my Ute guide walked over to me and again looked into my eyes. 'Who is this man?' I kept asking myself. 'Surely he must know what I'm going through, but I haven't said a word about it to him. Not a word.' He stared a long while, and then reached out and lifted his arms to pick me up. I never once resisted or flinched, but rather found myself melting into his hold. I trusted completely, as he walked me to the center of this three foot deep pool of water, always keeping me above the surface. Slowly, slowly, with my eyes closed, I called to Haeb in silent prayer: 'This is for you, dear stepfather. This is the comfort, the joy, the release I send you, from my body to yours.' And as I concentrated on these words, I felt myself being submerged, ever so gently, into that crystal clear, stunningly cool canyon water. It first enshrouded my feet, then my legs, my back, my hands, my arms, my heart, and finally it swirled around and embraced my throat. 'Here is the comfort, Haeb; soak it in.'

In this water, the man never let go of me, but only immersed my body completely, as if it were a baptism into the elements. He then lifted me as carefully and walked to the other side of the pool, placing my feet back on the earth. I could find no words to say thank you, but only stared into him with all the love of my heart.

We lay on the rocks and dried off, taking a brief rest before continuing what fast became our pilgrimage in this holiest of lands. During my rest on the rock, I continued to sit with Haeb, offering him the peace I had found on this day. Yes, this was the first time I had felt such solace in the two years of battling with the cancer. Sweet was the serenity I sent to his hospital room, praying with him, lifting him.

We walked for many hours, then, up the slickrock, up the canyon walls, feeling its skin and bone, flesh and soul, breathing new life into us through our feet. At the top of the canyon, the air was tenderly silent, palpably still. I hardly breathed, as I tiptoed most softly across its horizon. Our guide led us to a small cavern and only pointed, never uttering a word, to an old stone hearth where arrowheads, mortar and pestles all sat upon its base, speaking of earlier peoples' lives and witnessing to their daily work in these plateaus. Looking across the canyon to the other ridge, I could see many more pictographs etched into the rock wall, probably thousands of years old. They depicted the myriad experiences of the Ute culture: images of cooking, of worshipping, dancing, marriage, birth, and death. I revelled in this tapestry, seeing one moment upon the next as a gradual journey of the spirit in humankind. In this light, death was not something to be feared but rather revered as yet another stage of life. With love and support in community, I realized that even death could become a blessed and celebrated threshold.

I sent every one of these images to Haeb in his hospital room – every line, every curve, every dance, every connection. I shared with him this revelation about death – that it was a passing, a crossing over, illusory in any sort of finality or separation. I told him it was all right to let go, when he was ready, for we were all embracing him; and then I fell into the deepest stillness, holding Haeb in the Light as I gazed upon this beloved wilderness, ancient and free.

Dusk enveloped us, high above the canyonlands, as the sinking light cast orange shadows upon this inner world. A hawk then swept down so gracefully, so very close to my body, captivating my attention and awakening me as I lifted my head to watch it soar. Such freedom I had never felt before: we flew together, and I was tremendously lighter, even airborne, in that setting sun. Something had drastically shifted, and all of us knew it. I looked to my guide and he was already glancing at me. We smiled and stood slowly, then descended the cliff without ever a word. At our trail's end, I had only one question to ask: the time. Something in me wanted to mark this moment, tangibly, for I feared it might utterly dissolve if I didn't do so. It was 8.00 p.m., and the world had somehow transformed in that orange light.

Rosie and I slept soundly in the tent, until we were wakened by laughing coyotes with the morning sunrise. I zipped open the door to breathe in the new day and found, much to my surprise, a small glass bottle holding a single rose – white with red borders, this particular variety, a favorite of mine, is named 'Fire and Ice'. My heart stopped, for the message could not have come more clearly to me: Haeb had died. I thought of all the years he had left me a single rose (and so often this type) by my bedside, an act of love and appreciation as he shared the treasures of his beautiful garden. And now, he was the gardener in the wilderness, returning to me the care I'd given him the day before in the canyon. He was walking across the earth now, leaving his flowers all the way home.

We quickly went to find a phone to call Mother, who was frantic by the time I reached her. 'Thank God you called! I didn't know how to find you, honey. Haeb died last night. It was the strangest thing. He'd been struggling all yesterday morning, but around mid-day, he just turned and began to stare out the window – with the most peaceful look in his eyes. He even smiled several times, and seemed to be in a state of utter bliss as he looked out there. Then he went to sleep.'

'What time did he die, Momma?' was all I could ask, in utter awe of such affirmation. 'Ten,' she replied. 'That is two hours later than my moment of revelation,' I thought to myself. 'But wait! There is a two-hour time difference between here and Philadelphia. My 8.00 was his 10.00.' Meticulous.

I never again saw our guide after this pilgrimage to the Moab desert. In fact, if it weren't for Rosie, I would most certainly believe that this Ute man, walking and sharing his ages of wisdom with me, had been an illusion or a figment of my imagination. As she and I packed up our campsite to leave the orange slickrock, we discovered a cassette tape sitting on the driver's seat of my car – a homemade selection of music which was entitled 'Close 2 Me', handwritten in black ink. I stared at this script for a long while, wondering what was intriguing me most about such a phrase. Clearly, it was the name of the first song in this compilation which must have taken hours to record. But it was the number '2' which stared back at me with enigmatic wonder. As in everything else I'd experienced with this stranger, I knew there was more to discern from this teacher who walked between the ancient and modern worlds.

Holding the cassette, I realized it slowly and said it carefully: 'He was my Shaman, Rosie. He took me to the gateway and led me between the worlds.' Anything I had ever read about Native American shamanism came rushing in, as I stared trance-like onto the paved road stretching out before us. Rosie's curiosity got the better of her: she took the cartridge from my hands and slipped it into the cassette player. 'Gonna Run Away' were the first three words sung emphatically on this soundtrack. Run away. Yes, I had tried. I hit 'Pause', wanting to digest what was happening – and what was being said between the lines – as quickly as I could. I hit 'Play' again.

The lyrics of each song took me deeper into the mystery of what had just transpired in the desert. U2 – yet another interesting band name to come along on this inner journey – sang:

> If I could through myself set your spirit free
> I'd lead you all the way
> See you break, break away
> So let it go –

Crosby, Stills and Nash cautioned, 'and it gets harder as you get older/farther away, as you get closer.' Fleetwood Mac asked, 'And do you know how to pick up the pieces and go home?' More and more voices filled our car, as we drove forward with beating pulse and varying meters: 'Wavelength'; 'Closer 2 U'; 'Running on Empty'; 'Black Widow'; 'Southern Cross'.

Closer and closer I moved toward the profound message I'd been given in the canyon. I recounted my state of mind prior to leaving Boulder – anxious, distracted, and confused as I longed to be in two places at the same time. Rather than turning east to Haeb's bedside, I'd headed left, off the beaten and expected track and towards the western sky. As if called there by this Shaman, who was surely a mediator between the ordinary and the supernatural (Ricketts 1983: 89), I was escorted to the gateway and invited into a sacred state where I could be at both places simultaneously. All of this – and only by letting go. It was, after all, a message of holy surrender.

The dualities of this quest suddenly appeared astounding to me. The passage into the canyon was, at the same time, a passage to Haeb's hospital room; whereas I'd felt guilty for 'abandoning' my stepfather and rushing to the desert for peace, I'd actually been guided to such a place where I could more deeply connect to him and more prayerfully assist him in his transition and passing from one world to the next. Time, as well as distance, became illusory, for not only had two places become one in this altered world; two different times were suddenly the same moment, as I noted the hour Haeb passed away.

In this mystical world, a haven of unity and connection, the inversions and reflections were everywhere I turned, even to the most graphic of details: my eyes were Haeb's; his throat was mine. Indeed, the mysterious rose at my tent's door was rich with dual meanings. As the emblem of my stepfather's most cherished gift to me, its colors spoke of fire and ice, two opposite elements combined in one magnificent symbol of then and now, here and there. All melded together with remarkable lucidity, as my companion – yet another Rose – stayed 'Close 2 Me', bearing witness to the magic of Moab unfolding.

U2's concluding lyrics spoke to my condition as Rosie and I turned out of the last winding canyon road, our exodus from the desertscape, and headed east:

> And you know it's time to go –
> And you hunger for the time, time to heal,
>   desire time,
> And your earth moves beneath your own dream landscape.
> On Borderlands we run –

This healer had taught me many things with hardly a word ever spoken. He had accompanied me to the borderlands with exquisite grace, ancient power and deepest light at a time when I hungered for it profoundly; when I was most open, nearly desperate, to receive the lessons; and when the dreams and the reality blurred together, in willing suspension, so that new vision could be gathered in this most liminal of lands. Then he offered me the gift of music to keep the breath and spirit of that journey alive, even to this day.

What I have realized in the years since that odyssey is that while the Shaman was there to lead me further into the mystery, it was God the Trickster at work who shook me out of the patterns of my daily life, beyond all borders, and far away to the land of the excluded. This revelation has come from many years of spiritual reflection, critical inquiry, and most directly from teaching mythology to my college students. As a central figure of many cultural literary traditions, the Trickster (who I've most always recognized as the coyote in Native American creation myths) is the character who causes confusion, produces chaos and sometimes even death. He leads others to the threshold, takes them to the gateway, and then, quite daringly, crosses over the border with them so that they can see things they might have been unable to perceive or grasp otherwise. As a 'boundary crosser', he intends to confuse the distinctions of inner and outer, to blur the clearly defined lines of the real and the illusory, so that we can transcend ordinary existence (Hyde 1998: 6-8).

Indeed, William Hynes' analysis of the Trickster's complexity illustrates how this character has the unique capacity not only to disorder and disassemble things, but to violate social taboos and break rules and traditions so that we will be shaken loose from our habits of understanding in our daily lives (Hynes 1993a: 40). The trick, therefore, is not arbitrary or erratic at all, but an intricate design which provokes us to break free from our world in order to see life anew.

Confounded by the chaos in my life back in 1988, I had felt compelled to break the rules and head west, unable to fulfill my expectations and commitments to family and school any longer. I'd run empty and simply had nothing left to give. I'd surrendered and accepted my own failure. But in retrospect, I see things through a different lens today. The Trickster was immersing me in the turmoil and conflict which provoked me to leave my exam, my obligations, and the face of death itself as I shook loose, not knowing why: as I had said to my mother, 'I'll tell you when I get back.' And I continued to violate taboos, for never would I have dared to follow a stranger into a strange land as I did when I agreed to let the Ute man take me to an unknown destination in the canyon. It seemed to be an act of desperation, of emptying out, and yet I see now that God was at hand, a Trickster who inevitably guided and protected me in the most extraordinary and unexpected of ways. To the meticulous details – even to a Shaman in Gap jeans – I was being shown that this inner/outer journey was drawing me to the source of the gap – the gap between the worlds – where healing and vision could come if I remained open to listening and willing to surrender.

This was the leading – a trick which saved me, body and soul. As evidenced by Trickster figures across many cultures, it is ultimately the 'Trick' which stretches us, revitalizes us, and reaffirms our belief systems (Hynes 1993b: 207-12). During this walk among the ancestors, I learned, most indelibly, that death and birth were merely two sides of the same picture: the gate, the passageway, the passing. Dualities coalesced in blessed, prophetic oneness. Out of this revelation came a stronger connection to Haeb, superseding any communication I'd ever experienced with him, and a stronger bond with the earth, the heavens, the ancestral spirits dancing among us, and the ages of humankind still to be born. Fear melted as the web of sacred relations expanded and multiplied. At the crossroads of Moab, I found that I was not in the illusory land of the excluded but rather deep in the heart of God and amidst the resurrection of faith through loving connection. I was renewed and ready to sing with my Shaman all the way home.

Some days, I think about the coyotes who woke us on the morning I discovered Haeb's rose and wonder if they were telling me the Trickster was at work all along; their laughter – such distinct peals of laughter and the call of the wild – still reverberates inside me, as I recount the exceptional details of this unconscious errand into the wilderness. As the divine shapeshifter and situation invertor (Hynes 1993a: 36-7), God the Trickster had surely created some intricate magic in this visionary realm of slickrock and sage.

On other days, I ponder if Haeb himself had been orchestrating all of this from his hospital bed, sending the Shaman to me and letting go only when he saw *my* transformation in the desert. I recollect his own fascination with ancient history, his avid reading about the earliest cultures, and even his last trip to Cancun – land of the Mayan healers – before coming home to die. Perhaps he had already connected to this path of spiritual healing and sent me to Moab, through our unique wave of communication, as he lay in his sanitized and anaesthetized hospital bed seeking release from the twentieth-century medical industry and transformation with the ancestors.

I remain open to the possibilities. And still, I continue to weave the tapestry of this journey as I revisit each step through sacred memory, year after year. The mysteries there remain full and deep, as the creative potential granted to me by the divine Trickster is boundless and free. Anything was possible between the worlds of death and life, fire and ice, where two became one, ever moving 'Closer 2 Me'.

What I have ultimately discerned from this adventure is that we clearly cannot always understand our leadings; in fact, they may at times seem ludicrous, even self-indulgent or irresponsible. But God the Trickster, in all of the divine's many forms and callings, is looming large out there as 'the lords of the in-between' (Hyde 1998: 6), awaiting our courage to listen, our willingness to act, and our faith to surrender. No prophetic message could have been taught to me more poignantly than this one, as I listened and moved aimlessly through the desert – that illusory land of the excluded which transformed into a beloved temple, the holiest of rocks. My faith was renewed and solid as the walls of the canyon, returning home with a rose in the loving presence of God.

⊙ This essay is dedicated to my beloved stepfather, M. Gene Haeberle Esquire

References

Bright, W. *A Coyote Reader*. Berkeley: University of California Press, 1993.

Erdoes, R. and Ortiz, A. *American Indian Myths and Legends*. New York: Pantheon Books, 1984.

Hyde, L. *Trickster Makes this World*. New York: Farrar, Straus & Giroux, 1998.

Hynes, W.J. 'Mapping the Characteristics of Mythic Tricksters: a heuristic guide.' In Hynes, W.J. and Doty, W.G., *Mythical Trickster Figures: contours, contexts, and criticisms*. Tuscaloosa: University of Alabama Press, 1993a: 33-45.

Hynes, W.J. 'Inconclusive Conclusions: tricksters – metaplayers and revealers.' In Hynes, W.J. and Doty, W.G., *Mythical Trickster Figures: contours, contexts, and criticisms*. Tuscaloosa: University of Alabama Press, 1993b: 202-18.

Radin, P. *The Trickster: A Study in American Indian Mythology*. New York: Schocken Books, 1973.

Ricketts, M.L. 'The Shaman and the Trickster.' In Hynes, W.J. and Doty, W.G. *Mythical Trickster Figures: contours, contexts and criticisms*. Tuscaloosa: University of Alabama Press, 1993: 87-105.

Trickster and the Power of Paradox

Nat Kuhn

I didn't have Care of Meeting that morning, I'm glad to say. The small group of Friends with whom I habitually 'shared my concerns' about the quality of our vocal ministry were all aghast: 'Were there any newcomers there this morning?' 'I guess we won't be seeing them again!'

It was a Meeting for Worship during what we in the US called the 'Gulf War'. A woman who had been attending meeting for a number of months and was active on the Peace and Social Action Committee of our university-town meeting stood up, told us that she had been deeply affected by an article in the *Wall Street Journal*, showed us her copy, and started to read it. She hadn't gotten far before a seasoned Friend, I believe a former clerk of the Worship and Ministry Committee, interrupted her, saying 'I don't think it's appropriate to read newspaper articles during Meeting for Worship.'

A young man who had been coming for a few weeks piped up with, 'I think she should be allowed to do whatever she wants.'

Finally, another Friend rose and asked us to return to silent worship, holding all of those who had spoken in the Light. Needless to say, those of us who knew what should and shouldn't happen during Meeting for Worship were in despair. 'It's bearable for us, I suppose, but what if it were your first meeting?' We felt both pressed to protect the newcomer and powerless to do so.

About a year later, I was talking with a woman who'd been coming to our meeting for some time, one of those people who drops seemingly from nowhere and infuses some aspect of meeting life with new vigor. The subject turned to our experience in our very first meeting for worship, and she said, 'Well, in my first meeting, someone stood up and read an article from the *Wall Street Journal*.' We all blanched and someone must have said, 'I'm amazed you ever came back!' With great feeling, she said something like, 'No, it was wonderful, that's *why* I came back. I had a faculty meeting in my department the next day, which I had been dreading, so I wound up coming to meeting. There was something about the care that everyone had for each that I found very moving, and I was able to go into the faculty meeting with a whole different attitude. It was a really important experience for me.'

And with that, it became an important experience for me as well, reminding me that I am not the final authority on what makes a Meeting for Worship good, or on anything else for that matter. God is indeed a Trickster, who is willing to help us out by lovingly whacking us on the side of the head with our own expectations – as many times as it takes us to 'get it'.

It has not immunized me against the hand-wringing we fall prey to over the 'quality of our vocal ministry', but it's given me some detachment that I didn't have before. I've trotted this story out enough that when I ask Ministry and Counsel, 'Did I tell you about the *Wall Street Journal* article?' they all nod energetically, hoping to redirect my energies.

If God is a Trickster, and if we are to do God's work on earth, then the syllogism suggests that we are called to be Tricksters, too. Some of my very favorite Quaker stories come out of this strand of our experience. A non-Quaker teacher of mine told me one, which took place at Swarthmore College several years before his arrival there in the early fifties. Fifth Day Meeting was still compulsory, and to help pass the time for those who were not by nature drawn to silent worship, a few students had set up a betting pool around who would offer vocal ministry on a particular day. You could place a bet on Rufus Jones, though he ministered so frequently that the odds were short and you wouldn't win much if he spoke. On the other hand, there were a number of faculty members who were infrequent ministers and if you were fortunate in your wagers you could do quite well.

Eventually word of this got to the college administration, who of course put a stop to it – in a quietly dramatic way. It happened that one Thursday morning, one after another, a string of infrequent ministers rose and each delivered a brief message! The faces of those who ran the betting pool must have become more and more ashen as they totaled up their losses; at rise of meeting they were invited to the Dean's Office to talk things over.

Nothing ruins a great story more effectively than trying to explain it, but I can't resist trying to figure out why I love this story so much. To me there is something quintessentially Quaker about relying not just on moral hectoring to make a point (though we do more than enough of that), but letting the natural consequences of a person's actions speak to them about their behavior. And when 'natural consequences' aren't quite sufficient, we're willing to give things a little bit of a push to help them along. If that push involves bending the 'rules' of Quaker worship a bit, well, there are people around who won't stand in the way of a truly great story. We may not all have an 'inner Trickster', but enough of us do.

The more I think about this subject, the more I realize that almost all my most cherished Quaker stories have a Trickster aspect. The best example is probably the famous exchange in which William Penn, son of an Admiral in the Royal Navy and recent Quaker convert, reportedly asked George Fox whether he could continue to wear the sword traditional to young men of his station. Who but the Trickster-inspired could have replied, 'Wear it as long as thou canst.'? This is truly a case of 'less is more': no sermon could confront us so effectively with the fact that our actions, to be meaningful, need to come from our own Inner Teacher rather than simply conforming to a social standard – whether that standard is set by 'the world' or by the Quaker community.

To me, the final piece of Tricksterism in this story is that there is absolutely no confirmation in the historical record that it ever actually happened. Which is of course not to say that it didn't, either. I used to share the disappointment that I've seen on the faces of many Friends when they first hear that this beloved story is 'unattested'.

Now that very uncertainty adds another layer of irony: this story captures, in my spiritual universe, some very real essence of Quakerism. Was that essence there with Fox? Did it get snuck in later? Did we need this message so much that we acquiesced in its invention? It's a lesson on the divergence that sometimes occurs between historical veracity and spiritual truth.

Why is it important to me that God can be a Trickster, and that we are called to be Tricksters too? I think it has to do with the power of humor and paradox to remove us from the idolatry of the well-worn ways of thinking that we fall prey to as individuals, as a culture, and as a religious body. When paradox works, it offers us a trap door out of our prison of words, and into the mystery that is the essence of the divine. And that is something truly worth celebrating.

To Prosper You and Not to Harm You

Seren Wildwood

> There is in me
> A life not become ...
> A fire not kindled,
> Glowing like a lone
> And passionate sentinel
> Awaiting the dawn.
>   (Gateley 1996: 109)

God has, I believe, a life for each of us. This life is one to be lived close to God, enfolded in God, imbued with God. But when we sin our sin separates us from God, and although God calls us close, we remain separate until we can find the way back. Were the way back to God easy, we would have taken it years ago. Only by 'tricking' us, by leading us on paths we would not ourselves have chosen, can God bring us close again.

Vocation is not a word much used in Quaker writing. Neither 'vocation' nor 'calling' appear in the index of *Quaker faith & practice*, the book of discipline of Britain Yearly Meeting. Friends heed 'promptings', follow 'leadings', receive 'guidance', and act under 'concern', but rarely do we express such motivations as vocational. Why is this? Perhaps we take for granted Luther's assertions that true faith in God is to be worked out in the difficult circumstances of ordinary life and that all walks of life in which it is possible to live honestly are divine vocations? Perhaps vocation in this sense has become the *sine qua non* of Quaker life and is not, therefore, up for consideration? Or perhaps for us, as for the wider society we live in, the concept has been so secularized that 'everyone regards himself as entitled to speak of his calling without any reference to God' (Davies 1983: 602), as a result of which we consider vocation as irrelevant to matters spiritual?

But what does an individual Friend do when she feels herself called by God to a particular way of life? How does she test her calling in a faith community unfamiliar with the vocabulary of vocation? And where does she turn when the Caller appears to have turned Trickster and seems to have invited her to 'a life not become'? Britain Yearly Meeting is now seeing a revival of the use of meetings for clearness, but ten years ago all I had were the stories of calls from God in the Bible and in the writings of early Friends. I read these to try to discern how it might feel to be called by God and how to stay faithful, but the experience of others, however helpful, is not the benchmark against which Friends judge their sense of calling. The principle which underlies our way of life is 'the call to trust our own deepest experiences' (Quaker Women's Group 1986: 3), and I only found the way to my vocation when I finally followed the difficult and painful path through the Trickster's terrain, when I learned to listen deep within, to feel and release the hurts that had been buried there for many years, and to let God love me through and through.

> Women's distinctive sin is self-contempt. This self-hatred is symbolised by and centred on the body ... Pride plays a part ... for the woman discounts herself as part of Creation and assumes that the rules of divine love do not apply to her. Love is there for everyone else, but not for her ... [Separating] the strands of her sinfulness ... is delicate and gentle work, for sin always involves hurt: hurt of others, hurt of God, hurt of ourselves (Guenther 1992: 135-7).

'A *life not become*'

When I married in 1988 I knew with unfailing certainty that God had called me to marriage and motherhood. In the early months of our married life I felt and expressed in my prayers enormous gratitude for the husband God had given me, and I waited eagerly for the first signs of pregnancy so that I could begin the rest of the work that I believed God had for me. But the months of waiting turned to years, and no sign came. I met the inevitable questions from friends and family with good humour, and found a measure of consolation in a midwifery training I had wanted to undertake for years. However, the joy of being surrounded by mothers and babies only served to heighten the pain of my own infertility, and increasingly the innocent enquiries from clients caused unprofessional tears to well up in my eyes. I moved into other work; well-meaning friends suggested that I get a pet or become involved in some other caring work, but deep down I knew that God wanted me to wait, to keep myself free of other commitments, so that I could give myself wholeheartedly to the task to which God had called me.

I did, however, finally yield to the gentle pressure to seek help, even though in my heart of hearts I knew that this was somehow 'not right', although I could not at the time articulate my reasons for believing this. In the spring of 1996 I telephoned my homeopath to make an appointment to discuss my infertility. When I had last seen her in 1993 we had touched on the matter, but I was then in the final year of my course and in no hurry to become pregnant. That evening I wrote in my journal:

25.4.1996

I have worked myself into quite a state today: I had somehow been relying on J—[my homeopath] to 'fix' me, once I finally swallowed my pride sufficiently to contact her, but she is taking a sabbatical and is not seeing clients for another six months. I felt quite shocked and trembly after we had spoken. I cried and felt good for nothing. But I have to admit that, ultimately, I am powerless in this. It is not up to me. My ambition has nothing to do with it. Paul and the author of the letter to the Hebrews bring some comfort:

> None of the trials which have come upon you is more than a human being can stand. You can trust that God will not let you be put to the test beyond your strength, but with any trial will also provide a way out by enabling you to put up with it (1 Cor. 10: 13, JB).

> Do not lose your courage because it brings with it a great reward. You will need perseverance if you are to do God's will and gain what he has promised (Heb. 10: 35-6, Good News Bible and JB).

But I am hanging on by my fingernails to the faith that this is not just some empty flannel written without experience.

5.6.1996

I found a fragment of a 'catechism' coming to me:

> What are my priorities?
> My priorities are prayer, rest and recreation, and the work that God has made me to do.
> What is the work that God has made me to do?
> Reclaiming my soul.

'Give me children, or I will die.'

That night, at quite the 'wrong' phase of my cycle, I began to bleed, lightly at first, then after a few days heavily and painfully. They say that a little learning is a dangerous thing: by the end of the week I had convinced myself that this was the start of an early menopause, and had worked myself into a fearful state:

11.6.1996, 12.40 a.m.

I howl and howl; I am inconsolable. It is late and I am alone. This is the pits. I feel betrayed, angry, let down, despairing. I blame myself (for marrying the man I did), Alex (for wasting so many of our married years doubting his ability to be a father when we could have been working together to have a family, and now it's too late), God (for letting it all happen, for not making a world that works perfectly), religion (for telling us that God is all-powerful and loving: no loving deity who was all-powerful could possibly let its creatures suffer like this), my parents (for teaching me such independence that I didn't seek help for infertility years ago), the world (for going to sleep at night), all my friends (for being asleep when I need them), etc, etc. I pray for forgiveness, for healing, for comfort, but no comfort comes. Where is everyone? Where is God? The slightest little thing upsets me: a spider crawls across the carpet and approaches the bed – I collapse into another fit of howling: 'Go away! Go away! I don't want a spider in my bed! Go away!' Eventually, I get it onto a piece of paper and remove it from my vicinity, but I come back to bed still crying.

> Save me, God, for the waters
> have closed in on my very being.
>   I am sinking in the deepest swamp
> and there is no firm ground.
> I have stepped into deep water
>   and the waves are washing over me.
>   (Ps. 69: 1-2, JB)

> I cry to God in distress,
> I cry to God and he hears me.

>   In the day of my distress I sought the Lord;
> all night I tirelessly stretched out my hands,
>   my heart refused to be consoled.

> Through the night I ponder in my heart,
>   as I reflect, my spirit asks this question:
> Is the Lord's rejection final?
>   Will he never show favour again?

Is his faithful love gone for ever?
Has his word come to an end for all time?
Does God forget to show mercy?
In anger does he shut off his tenderness?
(Ps. 77: 1-2, 6-9, JB)

I am filled with love when the Eternal One[1] listens
to the sound of my prayer,
when he bends down to hear me as I call.

The bonds of death were all round me,
the snares of Sheol held me fast;
distress and anguish held me in their grip,
I called on the name of the Eternal One.

Deliver me, Eternal One, I beg you.

The Eternal One is merciful and upright,
our God is tenderness.
The Eternal One looks after the simple,
when I was brought low he gave me strength.

My heart be at peace once again,
for the Eternal One has treated you generously.
He has rescued me from death, my eyes from tears,
and my feet from stumbling.
I shall pass my life in the presence of the Eternal One,
in the land of the living.

My trust does not fail even when I say,
'I am completely wretched.'
(Ps. 116: 1-11, JB)

In peace I lie down and at once fall asleep,
for it is you and none other, Eternal One, who make me
rest secure.
(Ps. 4: 8b, JB)

---

[1] These quotations in my journal entry follow the Jerusalem Bible translation except that I substituted 'the Eternal One' for 'Yahweh' where the Hebrew is יהוה

I fall into a troubled sleep around 3 a.m.

12.6.1996

Yesterday I started to cry as I woke. Unable to stop crying, although I tried to get on with the day, I drove up to Woodbrooke [the Quaker college in Birmingham, where my husband was Friend-in-Residence for two terms] to find Alex.

Overnight I had a dream of statues of the Madonna. They were all different styles – some porcelain, one rough clay. I was clumsy, and broke one lifting it up. I broke another, and was upset – they were precious to me, but I felt that I would break every one I touched. I didn't dare touch the rest, in case I broke them too.

[Later] Alex has brought me home, as I am in pain again. I feel too tired to drive, and had left it too late to get a train that would connect with the last bus home. I feel reassured by his company, glad to be home, quietly sure that I must take things easy. No more heroics with five carrier bags of shopping. What are my priorities, again? 1. Prayer. 2. Rest and recreation. 3. The work that God has made me to do. Precisely! No mention there of heroics with shopping bags, housework, digging gardens, moving piles of rocks. Just take it easy. Alex will have to go back to Woodbrooke in the morning, but I feel better knowing that he will keep in touch more to see how I am.

13.6.1996

The pain is bearable when I lie down, makes sitting uncomfortable, and makes walking difficult unless I decide to ignore it and push on. I wonder whether this is the necessary shove I need to make me finally seek the help I need about infertility.

Before he left Alex and I talked about the Madonna dream: two broken statues; two lost pregnancies [an abortion when I was 18 and a miscarriage, which I felt I caused, at 25]. Carelessness, clumsiness; I didn't know what I was doing. I want to acknowledge my guilt and ask forgiveness. The sense in the dream of not daring to touch any more statues/pregnancies, in case I break them too: my body hasn't dared get pregnant for fear I would reject it/ruin it/lose it. It is time to face what I did, make amends, and allow the forgiveness and innocence that God offers.

19.6.1996
This afternoon I went to the Lady chapel of Gloucester Cathedral and knelt and prayed to say I am sorry for having rejected and been careless of the gift of life in the past. Now I feel ready to start again. I can't undo what was done, but I can make a fresh start. Vaclav Havel described hope as 'anchored somewhere beyond its horizon' (quoted in Quilley and Quilley 1996: 9), and although nothing has changed (I am still bleeding, still in pain), I feel as if I have been given my hope back.

> Oh Lord, I thank you
> For the cool and rainy days
> In summer.
> Oh Lord, I thank you
> For the glimpse of the sun
> In winter.
>
> Oh Lord, I thank you for despair,
> Which teaches me how good it is to hope.
> Oh Lord, I thank you
> For the trust I have in you.
>
> And when the sun comes out again
> I'll thank you for the golden glory of your world.
> And when it starts to snow again
> I'll thank you for the gleaming beauty of this land.
> And when I know your joy again
> I'll thank you for the peace within my heart.
> (McLeish 1996: 39)

'The darkness of God'

> I said to my soul, be still, and let the dark come upon you
> Which shall be the darkness of God.
>
> (Eliot 1944: 24)

17.6.1996

At a Quiet Day on the theme of the spirituality of the desert. We are invited at the start to draw ourselves, and I draw a desert and the words: 'Barren like the desert sands. "With my whole being I thirst for God, the living God."' In the silence that follows this exercise I get the words, 'Thank you for my grief'.

22.6.1996

The Talmud says that a dream uninterpreted is like a letter left unopened.

> 'Are not interpretations of dreams from Elohim?' [Gen. 40: 8], that is – God; the gods/goddesses; the divine realm; another part of our consciousness (Cooper 1991: 18).

So I sit with the dream I had ten days ago. I cut three images of the Madonna and Child from old Christmas cards and stick them in my journal to meditate on them. I read Vera von der Heydt's 'Mary – Receptive Woman'. Of the Dogma of the Assumption, which was declared only in 1950, she writes:

> A wrong has been righted: woman, and with her the feminine principle, has been given her rightful place ... Jung called it the greatest event in the Church since the Reformation: Mary the woman who embodies soul, the feminine principle, has been recognized collectively. Individually one has to find one's own soul (von der Heydt 1991: 88-9).

What is the work I have been made to do? The reclamation of my soul.

> Loss of the soul is serious; primitive people believed
> that the soul then goes into the land of the dead; this
> means psychologically that the soul withdraws into the
> collective unconscious. The land of the dead is the land
> of the ancestors who have left unanswered questions,
> unresolved problems; the unredeemed past emerges
> clamouring for answers. When, if, a soul returns from these
> dark regions, it will be stronger than before (*Ibid.*: 85).

> The Church has treated women badly, we all know that.
> Not only woman, but the feminine principle – instinct,
> the body, nature – had always been suspect, but during
> the Reformation the figure of the Virgin Mary, woman's
> cherished light aspect, was removed and banished by
> Reformers and Protesters ... She represents so much of
> that which we do not want to know: the feminine, the
> soul, goodness (*Ibid.*: 86-7).

> The Virgin Mary: the Eternal Feminine who guides men
> and women through Hell and Purgatory to Paradise,
> into the experience of forgetting and forgiving, helping
> sinful women and men find repentance and redemption:
> … 'Our Lady of the Way' (*Ibid.*: 84).

And so I allow 'Our Lady of the Way' to lead me through this
Hell and Purgatory: listening to my body's messages, and very much
following my intuition about what to do about them, I put together
a programme of prayer, journalling, meditation, and bodywork (aro-
matherapy, exercise, early nights, castor oil packs, and diet):

> We must learn to trust that the symptoms in the body
> are often the only way that the soul can get our atten-
> tion. Covering up our symptoms with external 'cures'
> prevents us from 'healing' the parts of our lives that
> need attention and change (Northrup 1995: 42).

4.7.1996

I have been looking at the story of the woman with a flow of blood (Matt. 9: 18-22, Mark 5: 21-34, Luke 8: 40-8). While my month of continuous bleeding pales by comparison with her twelve years, I begin to get a glimpse of how she must have felt. In all three accounts Jesus says, 'Daughter, your faith has made you well'.

> [This story's] deepest significance can be understood only if we try to put ourselves in this anonymous woman's world. Constantly losing blood, she was chronically weak and weary ... Not a day went by that she did not realize that she was seen as cursed and contagious ... This woman lived under a harsh sentence: 'If a woman has a discharge of blood for many days, not at the time of her impurity ... all the days of the discharge she shall continue in uncleanness' (Lev. 15: 25-7). She was not allowed to enter any of the holy places of worship as long as her bleeding continued. She was considered ritually impure, a threat to the holiness of the entire community ... This unnamed woman is the ultimate symbol of woman's biology despised ... Jesus was on an urgent mission at the request of an imposing man. She was a bleeding, anonymous, no-account woman in a crowd of thousands. But she pushed ahead. It was a particularly grave risk for her deliberately to touch another person – and this was a holy man ... [Jesus] called her 'daughter' and commended her faith. He told her to go in peace.
>
> With one look, Jesus removed the woman's shame ... With one blessing, he proclaimed female bodies holy. By healing one woman, he touched us all – all of us who have been taught that our body's rhythms are shameful and unclean, rather than a celebration of connection to life's cycles and seasons, to fertility and abundance and hope (Hollyday 1994: 189-92).

6.7.1996

As I fell asleep last night I remembered that the woman told Jesus 'the whole truth' (Mark 5: 33). On the level of spirit I am haemorrhaging through the cracks left between the whole truth and the level of truth on which I live. When she told the whole truth Jesus said, 'Daughter, your faith has made you well; go in peace, and be healed of your disease.' It is fear that stops me from living wholly truthfully. 'Do not be afraid; only have faith' (Mark 5: 36). Faith and fear are opposite tendencies: in fear I try to protect myself from censure, I make myself less than I am, I hide the parts of myself that I think will be unacceptable (weak, tired, muddled, needing); in faith I trust those around me enough to be the whole of who I am. And when I do that I regain my integrity. I become whole and well in spirit. Just as Jesus stopped to affirm the 'bleeding, anonymous, no-account woman' while on an urgent mission, I think this is about stopping to affirm the weakness, the tiredness, the muddle, the needs, the aspects of myself that have been 'of no account' in my seemingly urgent, important, action-packed life. The separation of holy=strong=important=reliable=rational and unholy=weak= marginalized=unreliable=irrational is dysfunctional. Of course, I have known this with my mind, but I have not been living it out. But now I come to recognize the holiness there is in loss, in women's bodies, in our cycles, in the barely articulate groping for words long denied.

Dear Loving Truth, May I see clearly that which is. May I have faith to tell the whole truth. May I turn my thoughts, and words, and actions to align myself with the deepest Truth. And may your Light show me my darkness, that I may be healed. Amen.

'To be restored, our sickness must grow worse.'
18.7.1996

Yesterday I received the results of the various tests done to find the cause of the pain and bleeding. A very low oestradiol level may account for them, but at present nothing can be done about it because a routine smear test taken at the same time has revealed moderate dysplasia [precancerous changes to the cells of the cervix of the uterus]. For ten minutes I could hear the news as 'just factual information'. Then I had two minutes of 'I'm scared; hold me!' with tears. Then a deep sense of release and joy as I recognized the impetus I need to begin finally to take care of myself properly. As I walked home I noticed how blue the sky is, how beautiful the flowers are, how much I enjoy the call of seagulls. At home I sat with the news for a couple of minutes, and then knew that this was the incentive I needed to start the Gerson therapy [a rigorous naturopathic regime of diet, vegetable juices, supplements, and detoxifying treatments]. I did the first treatment last night: the pain went immediately, the bleeding stopped within two hours.

19.7.1996

I was so aware of my sense of vocation this morning, of living the truth I have been given: what I am here to do is to be a loving wife, and if God gives us children to love, then to love them, but not to worry or strive after them. And as I worked this morning, my vegetable juices made and drunk, baked potatoes cooking for lunch, I felt that this is finally becoming a happy home, something it has not been for years. As I get well (in spirit and in body) our home may once more become

> a place of friendliness, refreshment and peace, where God becomes more real to all who live there and to those who visit it (Britain YM 1995: 22.20).

Alex says he thinks we had this when we were first married, but that we have needed to journey somewhere else before coming back to it.

26.7.1996

Back from a Hebrew summer school on the subject of 'men and women': the whole thing turned out to be an ecclesial version of laddishness, all formal theological discourse (among the men), anything to keep the women – and, above all, any serious sharing about gender – out of the picture! But as we women shared disappointment, anger, and vision over cocoa in our kitchen, at mealtimes, in quiet moments, we affirmed each other and our sense of what could have been.

And I come home with a sense of the Divine older, deeper, and more all-encompassing than the Boys' Own, celibate, intellectual, Apollonian approach can touch. My Holy One came in the fragments of text that survived the clean-up operation of producing the canon we have been handed down as Scripture. My Beloved meets me in the quiet of the night, in desire and in completion, in sickness and in health, in inwardness and in action, in my pursuit of truth and in my surrender, in my fear and in my trust. My Heart embraces paradox, delights in it, generates it. Here is mystery, complexity, richness; 'a warm, moist, salty God' (Gateley 1996: 26); an earthy, open, subtle, inter-relating, weaving Heartbeat. And She is there in the text, in the richness and density of the Hebrew, in its allusions to and borrowings from older, lost tapestries of words and images and actions. She speaks to us when we stop to notice the accounts of (and to question the translations as) the voiceless 'whore', 'adulteress', 'damsel', 'woman of virtue'. She whispers through the hints of priestesses, goddesses, the women who knew and kept silent, passing Her on in songs, perfumes, embroideries. Deny Her and She will rise all the stronger to fill us, embrace us, guide us, to be our journey's beginning and its end, our movement and our stillness, to dazzle us and elude us. She is there. And we will seek Her out, and restore Her to the hearts of the women who hunger for Her flesh, thirst for Her milk, yearn for a whisper of Her name. She is there. In the poetry, in the sounds of Her names, in the word-pictures. She is there. She calls me, and I am Hers.

4.9.1996
Entries becoming rare: the healing process I am in is so physical, so demanding, that there is little time for journalling, exploring feelings or dreams: I am applying myself daily, hourly, to the rhythm of

becoming whole. Words are dropping away. My prayer times are wordless now, lying quiet, still, curled up, aligning myself with God: I feel God seeping into me like warmth seeps into bones after long exposure to the cold and wet. In Jonathan Sacks's *Faith in the Future* he tells the story of a rabbi who asks his son, 'Where does God live?' The son is confused and doesn't understand the question: 'God lives everywhere!' he exclaims, to which the rabbi replies that God lives where we let him in. Slowly I am letting God in. Slowly I am giving myself to God.

Trick or treat?

25.12.1996

Alex suggests that I 'start' journalling: 'start', because we are beginning to let in the possibility of a new stage of the journey. The results of a biopsy on my cervix were all clear. After five months on the Gerson therapy my skin looks young, supple; I have lost all the fat from around my hips and thighs that I put on over the last ten years; I have a daily rhythm, a rule to live by; I am calm and centred. And three weeks ago, on holiday in Scotland and the north-east, we made what we thought would be an overnight stop near Edinburgh. But on the Thursday afternoon the car broke down in the centre of Edinburgh, and was towed to a garage to await repair. We telephoned the garage on Friday morning, to be told that spare parts would have to be ordered: we had no option but to make an unscheduled extension to our stay. Our hosts were going away themselves for the weekend, but generously offered us the use of their home while they were away. So once they had left us, we returned to bed and made love. (Well, what else is there to do on a cold December morning?) That afternoon we walked in the Pentland hills, snow scrunching underfoot; we stopped to watch a fox in the twilight, then carried armfuls of wood home for the fire. We lit candles, and ate supper in front of our log fire, two blissfully happy peasants. A simple, blessed evening. And now, a week after my period was due, we wait. There is no single moment of knowing. Rather knowledge comes a snowflake at a time.

The still small voice whispers in our ears, and we wait quietly, calmly, to hear the words it may spell out in our hearts.

❁

8.9.1997

I am lying in bed with my milky-mouthed daughter lying blissed out beside me. (I have been wanting to write something since she was born just over a week ago, but until today, each time she blissed out I was too tired to do anything but crash out myself.) Thank you, God, for Hannah. Thank you for answering my prayers with such generosity. I feel blessed, exhausted, unreal, content, grateful. Blessed are you, Eternal One, our God, Ruler of the universe, who grants favours to the undeserving, who has granted me all kindness. I give thanks to you, Ruler of life and everlasting, who in mercy has returned my soul to me. Our trust in you is great. Blessed are you, Eternal One, our God, Ruler of the universe, who has granted us life and sustained us and brought us to this moment.

'All in the waiting'

> I said to my soul, be still, and wait without hope
> For hope would be hope for the wrong thing; wait
>   without love
> For love would be love of the wrong thing; there is yet faith
> But the faith and the love and the hope are all in the
>   waiting.
> (Eliot 1944: 24)

A fortnight before I conceived I took part in a Bible study weekend looking at 'barrenness' and the stories of Sarah, Rebekah, Rachel, Hannah, Manoah's wife (whose name we are not told), Elizabeth: all women who could not have children. But they all went on to have a child who played an important part in the unfolding story of God's relationship with 'His' people. Their 'barrenness' was, if you like, a way of creating suspense, of heightening the sense of anticipation, so that God's gifts and promises would be valued and not simply taken for granted.

The years of awful waiting, the times of hopelessness, gave me something after all. When I stopped struggling and let myself float to the bottom of the pond, there was, I discovered, a gift waiting in the darkness for me to find: the gift of my own soul.

Recently I watched a television interview with a gay man who had lived for ten years with HIV. Towards the end of the interview he said that if he could go back ten years and change his diagnosis he wouldn't do it, that living with HIV had made him a better person, and that he wouldn't change that for anything. I was moved and humbled by this quiet and unassuming insight into the meaning of suffering.

> The only wisdom we can hope to acquire
> Is the wisdom of humility: humility is endless.
>   (Eliot 1944: 23-4)

Postscript

At the age of fourteen months my beautiful baby, my longed-for daughter, my gift of God, was rushed to hospital for emergency surgery to remove part of a large malignant brain tumour. She has, as I write, recovered well from the surgery and is undergoing a course of chemotherapy, but the medical prognosis is not good.

Why, as I sit with this shocking reality six weeks later, do I not feel the hand of the Trickster at work in it? How is it that although there have been moments when I have felt the grief and wept, the predominant sense I have had since that night is an equanimity utterly different from the despair of the years waiting to conceive? Perhaps the Trickster's work is done: I was tested and accepted into my vocation, and it is not for me to specify the path thereafter. Today I feel only the presence of the God who suffers alongside us, who lives through such times as this with us, working to redeem us from fear; a God who loves us, upholds us, comforts us, inspires us. And while I am immeasurably grateful for the dedication and skill of the doctors and nurses who have cared for Hannah in the last six weeks, I have found myself putting my faith not in surgery nor in chemotherapy nor in good nursing, but in God.

Two of the one hundred and fifty or so cards that we received in the days following Hannah's surgery spoke particularly to me because they echoed what I was feeling and reassured me that God was indeed at work in this latest twist in the tale. The first quoted a verse from Isaiah:

> He will keep in perfect peace all those who trust in him, whose thoughts turn often to the Lord (Isa. 26: 3, Living Bible).

As the hospital staff were doing so much for Hannah in those first few days, all I could do was feed her and pray. In her distress she wanted to nurse as much for comfort as for food, and we had numerous feeds that lasted two hours or more: plenty of time to turn my thoughts to God; and I found that by keeping God as my bearing during these times I remained peaceful, untroubled by questions of 'why?' or 'what kind of God could allow …?', but able to focus calmly on Hannah and her healing.

The second card was a handmade one: Psalm 121 in Hebrew on the front, with an English translation inside, it echoed the sense I had of the Keeper: 'The Lord shall preserve thee from all evil: he shall preserve thy soul' (Ps. 121: 7, KJV). Having been given the gift of my soul, I was now being given the gift of reassurance that my soul is in God's keeping. And what I have discovered in the last few weeks is that what is important in the spiritual life, the life lived close to God, is not the events themselves, the crises, the times of calm, the triumphs and disasters, the 'successes' and 'failures', but my willingness in good times and in bad to turn my thoughts often to God and to trust myself and those I love constantly to God, what Brother Lawrence called 'the practice of the presence of God' (Blaiklock 1981: 35).

The experience of suffering is intensely personal, and no one can tell another person what their suffering means. But suffering can, if we choose to let it, bear us closer to God: the etymology of 'suffer' is 'sub-' (under, close to, up to, towards) and 'ferre' (bear). For me, suffering was what happened on the way back to God; it was how I experienced the 'trick' played on me by God to get round my sinful resistance, it was the means by which I was brought back.

When finally we come close to God, and look back on the journey we have taken, we see that the trick of suffering, if trick it was, was only the necessary means to bring us home.

'For I know the plans I have for you', declares the Eternal One, 'plans to prosper you and not to harm you, plans to give you hope and a future. When you call to me, and come and pray to me, I shall listen to you. When you search for me, you will find me' (Jer. 29: 11-13, NIV and JB).

Notes

The quotations used in the title and subtitles are as follows:
'To prosper you and not to harm you' is from Jeremiah 29: 11;
'A life not lived' is from the poem 'A dream I have not dreamt' by Edwina Gateley (1996);
'Give me children, or I will die!' is Rachel's cry in Genesis 30: 1;
'The darkness of God' is from 'East Coker' by T.S. Eliot (1944);
'To be restored, our sickness must grow worse' is from 'East Coker' by T.S. Eliot (1944).

References

Blaiklock, E.M. (trans.). *The Practice of the Presence of God: the conversations, letters, ways and spiritual principles of Brother Lawrence*. London: Hodder and Stoughton, 1981.
Britain Yearly Meeting of the Religious Society of Friends. *Quaker Faith & Practice: the book of Christian discipline of the Yearly Meeting of the Religious Society of Friends (Quakers) in Britain*. London: Britain Yearly Meeting, 1995.
Cooper, H. 'Dreaming up the Goddess'. In Pirani, A., ed., *The Absent*

Mother: restoring the Goddess to Judaism and Christianity. London: Mandala, 1991: 18-25.

Davies, R. 'Vocation.' In Richardson, A. and Bowden, J., eds., *A New Dictionary of Christian Theology.* London: SCM Press, 1983: 601-02.

Eliot, T.S. 'East Coker'. In *Four Quartets.* London: Faber and Faber, 1944.

Gateley, E. *There Was No Path So I Trod One.* Trabuco Canyon, California: Source Books, 1996.

Guenther, M. *Holy Listening: the art of spiritual direction.* London: Darton, Longman & Todd, 1992.

Hollyday, J. *Clothed with the Sun: Biblical women, social justice and us.* Louisville, Kentucky: Westminster John Knox Press, 1994.

McLeish, G. 'Celebration.' In von Ruhland, C., ed., *Prayers from the Edge: meditations for life's tough times.* London: Triangle, 1996: 39.

Northrup, C. *Women's Bodies, Women's Wisdom: the complete guide to women's health and wellbeing.* London: Piatkus, 1995.

Quaker Women's Group. *Bringing the Invisible into the Light: some Quaker Feminists speak of their experience.* London: Quaker Home Service, 1986.

Quilley, J. and Quilley, A. 'Seeds of Hope.' In *The Friend*, 10 May 1996: 9-11.

von der Heydt, V. 'Mary – Receptive Woman'. In Pirani, A., ed., *The Absent Mother: restoring the Goddess to Judaism and Christianity.* London: Mandala, 1991: 84-9.

The Contributors

Margery Post Abbott is currently writing and travelling in the ministry among Friends as a consequence of a call to ministry in 1991 and is a released Friend under the care of Multnomah Monthly Meeting in Portland, Oregon. Numerous articles, pamphlets and a book, *A Certain Kind of Perfection* (Pendle Hill, 1997) have emerged from her reflections on her faith. She is co-editing *The Historical Dictionary of Quakerism* (Scarecrow Press, 2002) and completing a book on Liberal Friends.

Jan Arriens is a British Quaker of Dutch descent. He was a diplomat in the Australian Foreign Service for 10 years, and has been a freelance translator for the past 20 years. He is the founder of LifeLines, whose members write to prisoners on Death Row in the United States. He was editor of *The Seeker* from 1992 to 1997 and author of a children's story, *The Knight and the Candle Flame*, published in 2000.

Kirsten Backstrom is a member of Multnomah Monthly Meeting in Portland, Oregon. She writes essays, fiction, and poetry. Her work has appeared in *Friends Bulletin* and *Friends Journal*, as well as in several anthologies and literary magazines. She is also involved in hospice work, and other areas related to death and dying.

Ben Pink Dandelion currently works at Woodbrooke Quaker Study Centre in England with the University of Birmingham, and for the Centre for Quaker Studies at the University of Sunderland. He came to Friends from an atheist and anarchist background but has lived a life 'accompanied by God' since a conversion experience on a Greyhound bus in 1986.

Chuck Fager was raised Roman Catholic in a military family and came to Friends as a Vietnam War CO. A longtime writer, reporter and editor, he has written much about Friends, both in his newsletter, *A Friendly Letter* (1981-1993) and numerous articles and books, including *Without Apology: the Heroes, the Heritage and the Hope of Liberal Quakerism*. From 1994-1997 he was staff for Pendle Hill's Issues Program. Now a member of State College, Pennsylvania Friends Meeting, Chuck teaches writing at Penn State University, and continues to work as a journalist and author.

Like the other contributors to this volume, **Nat Kuhn** has done many different things in his life, maybe they can weave them into a coherent whole, but he's not quite sure he can. These days he lives between Belmont and Falmouth, Massachusetts (USA), practises and teaches psychiatry, and is a member of Friends Meeting at Cambridge. He considers himself a 'post-universalist' Friend.

Marti Matthews, a member of Northside Friends in Chicago and active in Illinois Yearly Meeting, is a reluctant adventurer, changing directions and seeking the lighted path many times. She is the mother of two, author of a book, *Pain: the Challenge and the Gift*, and has edited newsletters for The New Call to Peacemaking, Illinois Yearly Meeting, and Quaker Volunteer Service and Witness Network. She is currently a counsellor at Triton Community College.

Gay Pilgrim, a Friend for 13 years, is a member of Warwickshire Monthly Meeting (UK). She is currently studying for a PhD on Contemporary Quakerism at Birmingham University and is an external tutor for Woodbrooke Quaker Study Centre.

Jane Orion Smith is a member of Victoria (BC) Monthly Meeting, Canada. A wide range of her poetry, articles, and papers have been published in various Quaker and non-Quaker publications and anthologies. A theatre artist and activist for years, until God turned her energies to Quaker ministry, she has served on many committees for Canadian Yearly Meeting, served as a Friend in Residence at Woodbrooke Quaker Study Centre in Britain, and researched James Nayler's writings at Pendle Hill in Pennsylvania as the Cadbury Scholar in Quaker Studies. Presently, she is the Co-ordinator of the Canadian Friends Service Committee.

Michele Lise Tarter is an Assistant Professor of English at The College of New Jersey. She has given numerous presentations about the early Friends' mystical experiences and has published several essays about transatlantic Quaker women's autobiographical writings. Her co-edited book, entitled *A Centre of Wonders; the body in North America* (Cornell University Press, 2001), includes her own essay on the physicality of early Quaker worship. Michele is a member of the Boulder Friends Meeting.

Although not from a Quaker family, **Seren Wildwood** grew up among Friends in Belfast, Northern Ireland, and was admitted into membership at the age of twenty-one. She has kept a spiritual journal for the past twenty-five years. A qualified naturopath and midwife, she currently edits biographies for an academic publisher.